THE
YEAR OF THE BEARS

THE
YEAR OF THE BEARS

By the Sports and Photo Staffs
of the Chicago Tribune

News Books International, Inc.
Indianapolis, Indiana 46220
1986

Front cover photo by Ed Wagner Jr.

Back cover photo by Bob Langer.

CONTENTS

Introduction

Images. They began in April with William Perry, "the Refrigerator," greeting Chicago with a wide, gap-toothed smile and a cheerful discussion of his even wider girth. And they concluded on the evening of Jan. 26, 1986, with Michael McCaskey, the grandson of George Halas, clutching a shiny, silver trophy as lovingly as the memory of Papa Bear.

Between the introduction of the Bears' secret weapon in Lake Forest and the justification of the "Super Bowl Shuffle" in New Orleans came a number of other indelible images.

There was the ugly first half against Tampa Bay in the opening game at Soldier Field. Boos cascaded down on the Bears as they left the field at halftime trailing the Bucs 28–17. The Bears came back, however, and won 38–28 to begin a 12-game winning streak and a love affair with a nation.

There was Jim McMahon swaggering into a disoriented huddle on a Thursday night in Minnesota. His back and leg ached, and his offense, behind back-up quarterback Steve Fuller, was trailing the Vikings 17–9. On the first play, he found Willie Gault for a 70-yard touchdown pass. On the second play, he found Dennis McKinnon for a 25-yard touchdown pass. A few minutes later, he found McKinnon again in the end zone. And, with the exception of a few who left the room to raid the refrigerator, a national television audience found a maverick superstar.

Then there was the Refrigerator, who is so big that his story took two weeks to unfold. In a convincing victory over the Super Bowl champion 49ers, coach Mike Ditka inserted the Bears' No. 1 draft pick, Perry, at running back as time expired. It was in response to a similar move San Francisco coach Bill Walsh made during the 49ers' victory over the Bears in the 1985 NFC championship game.

A week later, on "Monday Night Football" against Green Bay at Soldier Field, the pride of Aiken, S. C., and Inez and Hollie Perry came into full flower. Running out of Walter Payton's backfield and Ditka's fertile imagination, the Fridge blocked for two Payton touchdowns and ran for one himself. George Cumby, the Packer linebacker who twice tried to defy the laws of physics, still does not know what hit him.

Images. There was the barking in Dallas. Safety Dave Duerson and linebacker Otis Wilson arfed and woofed like dogs in the 44–0 victory over the Cowboys.

There was Dan Marino, his arm a streak of flesh tones and his receivers streaks of aquamarine on the floor of the Orange Bowl one December night. The Dolphins penned an asterisk on the Bears' record in the 13th game of the season.

There was Richard Dent sacking Giants' quarterback Phil Simms, and New York's Sean Landeta foul-tipping a punt in the Bears' first playoff game.

There was the wind-driven lakefront snow that provided a fitting exclamation point to yet another playoff shutout, this time against the Los Angeles Rams.

Images. There was the huge chip on the shoulders of the Bears, who, having lost a chance to play in Super Bowl XIX, carried it through an off-season, a season and into Super Bowl XX. And finally, there was Mike Ditka and Buddy Ryan—advertisements for creative tension at work—being hoisted onto those same shoulders.

It was the year of the Bears.

Gene Quinn
Sports Editor
Chicago Tribune

No contest: Bears the best!

By Don Pierson

New Orleans—This is as good as it gets. The Bears won the Super Bowl 46–10 in an awesome display of football encompassing all the joy and fury of an awesome season.

Their destruction of the New England Patriots was so complete it went beyond Super Bowl proportions and recalled only the record 73–0 victory by the Bears over the Washington Redskins in the 1940 National Football League championship game.

The Bears have a tradition that transcends Super Bowls, and Jan. 26, 1986, they ended years of frustration for their city and themselves and showed a nation they play even better than they talk or sing.

They simply blew your minds like they said they would.

After an early Patriots' field goal ruined their bid for an unprecedented third straight shutout, the Bears scored and scored until they reached the appropriate final number, stamping the "46" defense forever on NFL history.

They scored until the Cubs and White Sox had won the World Series, until the Black Hawks and Bulls had won world titles. They scored until all the doubts and fears of all those awful years were replaced by the deafening cheers of a Superdome crowd chanting "Let's Go Bears!"

Quarterback Jim McMahon, changing headbands more quickly than he changes plays, scored twice. Fullback Matt Suhey scored once. William "The Refrigerator" Perry scored after coach Mike Ditka called on him for a rollout pass he never got off.

Cornerback Reggie Phillips, subbing for injured Leslie Frazier, scored on an interception and defensive lineman Henry Waechter scored a safety.

McMahon answered the pressure of Super Bowl week with a near-perfect performance helped by a different kind of needle than his ballyhooed acupuncture treatments. He received a pain-killing shot in his sore rear end from team physician Dr. Clarence Fossier and was able to move away from the Patriot rush with ease. He was sacked only once.

"The Doc's needle worked," said trainer Fred Caito. "We went back to basic NFL treatment."

McMahon chose to wear several headbands out of the hundreds he said were sent to him.

"I decided to stick with the charities," said McMahon, who started with "JDF Cure" in honor of the Juvenile Diabetes Foundation; POW-MIA; and finished with "PLUTO" for former Brigham Young teammate Dan Plater, a cancer patient who is now in medical school at USC.

Only the cries of "Payton, Payton" went unanswered. Walter Payton failed to score, providing a harsh reminder that like their 18–1 record, not everything is perfect. He blocked, as usual, and ran hard, as usual, and said, as usual, that it wouldn't really sink in until next year.

"Right after we win it again," he said.

"I wanted to get Walter into the end zone," said Ditka. "But our plays are designed to score and I didn't know who had the ball."

"I feel very sad for No. 34," said McMahon. "I also would have liked to have seen a goose-egg up there. We could have got to 60 points, but we ran out of time."

This was the completion of a mission that Ditka said meant more to him than the Bears' and Chicago's last title in 1963 under George Halas.

"What you do in life by yourself doesn't mean as much as what you accomplish with a group of people," said Ditka.

"It's because of Mr. Halas that I'm here. I'm just trying to pay some dues."

They were paid in full in a little more than one devastating opening quarter, a microcosm of the season.

The Patriots scored first after Payton fumbled and the Bears scored twice after two Patriot fumbles, recalling Ditka's early-season vow never to be upstaged in anything in life.

"It didn't start out too well the first few series today," McMahon said. "The fumble [by Payton on the second play] was my fault. I made the wrong call. I put him in a bad situation."

"The game was never in question," said Ditka.

Quarterback Tony Eason could do no more than take five steps back and duck. When he got passes off, they looked like ducks. After three sacks and no completions in six attempts, the Patriots brought in veteran Steve Grogan, who finally got them a first down with 4:06 left in the half.

"We have to communicate," yelled middle linebacker Mike Singletary after the play. "They got a first down. It was ridiculous."

The Patriots had minus yardage until the third quarter. Grogan was sacked four more times and was intercepted twice.

Defensive coordinator Buddy Ryan broke down and admitted his defense was the best he had ever seen, a sentiment that provoked no argument.

"This was a 10," said Single-

SUPER BOWL

Walter Payton fumbles on the Bears' second play from scrimmage. The Patriots recovered at the Bears 19 and eventually kicked a field goal. (Tribune photo by D. Bierman)

tary. "Or at least a 9.999."

Ryan also broke down in a team meeting the night before the game.

"He told us, 'Win or lose, next week you guys are my heroes,'" said safety Dave Duerson. "By the time he was able to finish, his eyes filled with tears and they were running down his chin. His entire face was quivering. We stood up and gave him a standing ovation. Then Steve McMichael proceeded to destroy the chalkboard."

"We love each other. That's why we're so good," said McMichael.

Defensive end Richard Dent was the game's most valuable player because he was in on the Patriots' two early fumbles. After that, it was hard to see who was getting to the Patriot quarterback first.

Dent had a sack and a half. Otis Wilson had two. McMichael and Dan Hampton had one each. Wilber Marshall had a half and Waechter's safety provided the final two points.

Appropriately, defensive players scored the final three times. Phillips ran back an interception 28 yards for a touchdown and Perry's one-yard touchdown plunge preceded Waechter's safety.

Even referee Red Cashion scored for the Bears, proving it was a season that truly would have pleased Halas.

Cashion allowed Kevin Butler's third field goal on the last play of the half even though it was kicked against the rules.

McMahon, demonstrating a quick mind under all those headbands, threw a ball out of bounds before the referee had put it in play. The Bears were penalized, but Cashion should have run 10 seconds off the clock and not allowed the field-goal attempt.

Luckily, the Patriots couldn't complain about three points.

The Bears got going shortly after McMahon found receiver Willie Gault behind cornerback Ronnie Lippett for a 43-yard pass. The Bears isolated Gault on Lippett by flopping their for-

mation to get Gault away from Patriots' cornerback Raymond Clayborn.

It was a play-action pass that was a big part of the offensive game plan to take advantage of the aggressive Patriot defensive backs.

The Patriots came out passing because they figured they couldn't run. But the Patriots simply couldn't block anything.

"Dent was coming free. We knew we could be effective with different stunts until the well ran dry. It never did," said Singletary.

"Eason was throwing off his back foot. They should have rolled out. They made a mistake," said McMichael.

"The pocket collapsed on him. He was a little bit afraid to throw the ball and a little bit too timid to run it," said Hampton.

"His eyes were moving around," said Duerson. "John Hannah's eyes were moving. Brian Holloway's eyes were moving. The reason was we were creating havoc. They couldn't

Willie Gault clutches the ball after catching a pass for a 43-yard gain, setting up the Bears' first field goal. (Tribune photo by Bob Langer)

William Perry prepares to smash the ball to the ground after scoring a TD.
(Tribune photo by Charles Cherney)

Kevin Butler clenches his fist after kicking his second of three field goals.
(Tribune photo by Bob Langer)

block man. They couldn't block zone."

Eason fumbled when sandwiched by Dent and McMichael, leading to a field goal.

Then Craig James fumbled when he was picked up and tossed aside by Dent, leading to a touchdown by Suhey.

McMahon faked to Perry and followed a huge path for the touchdown that made it 20–3.

McMahon's perfect 60-yard pass to Gault early in the third quarter set up McMahon's second touchdown that made it 30–3 and ended any thoughts of respectability by the Patriots.

Payton ended up with 61 yards in 22 tough attempts, but the Bears established the run early with Suhey, who had 52 yards in 11 attempts.

"We knew if we could run, the play-action pass would open up because their cornerbacks eye the backfield so heavily," said center Jay Hilgenberg. "We knew if the line would keep our hats down and block like a run, it would open up big plays.

"Throughout the playoffs, teams have been taking Walter away from us."

Singletary said the only subtle difference in Ryan's "46" plans for this game was a "59" blitz that sent Singletary, Marshall and Wilson all after the quarterback.

But the rush of the front four was more than the Patriots could handle. They thought they were a better offense than the one that crossed midfield only twice against the Bears in a 20–7 loss Sept. 15. Ryan had said: "They better be better if they want to make a game of it."

The Bears called the Patriots a cheap bunch after proving they were unworthy competitors.

"I've got to be honest," said Singletary. "I thought New England was a lot better than what I saw today. They were trying to talk their way through us."

"We've never been a team to talk," said Duerson, who didn't mention barking. "When Les Frazier and Mike Singletary got

hurt, the Patriots were cheering and patting each other on the back. When their tight end [Lin Dawson] went out on a stretcher, our whole defense all clapped and cheered for him. They were a cheap organization that showed no class."

As usual, the Bears were mild-mannered and subdued afterwards, refusing to let that chip fall off their shoulders.

"You don't see any of us hyperventilating," said Duerson. "We knew we were the better team."

Now everybody should know it.

"People kept saying we weren't that great of a team," said Gault.

An article by a Boston columnist headlined "Chicago will choke again" was posted inside the Bears' locker room.

Chicago did the choking all right. And the Patriots did the gagging.

"No, it wasn't easy," said Singletary. "Maybe we made it look easy. But it wasn't easy."

Fullback Matt Suhey escapes a Patriot tackler to go in for the TD that gave the Bears a 13-3 lead. (Tribune photo by Bob Langer)

Bears' president Mike McCaskey talks with Walter Payton, Jim McMahon and Kevin Butler on the sidelines after the Bears' victory seemed assured. (Tribune photo by Bob Langer)

Tony Eason fumbles as he is sacked by Richard Dent. Dan Hampton (99) recovered the fumble, which led to Kevin Butler's tie-breaking field goal. (Tribune photo by Bob Langer)

Reggie Phillips scores a TD after a third-quarter interception. (Tribune photo by Charles Cherney)

Dennis Gentry catches a long pass and goes to the one-yard line to set up a second-half TD for the Patriots. (Tribune photo by Bob Wagner)

A delicious win for hungry city

By Bernie Lincicome

New Orleans—No more tears.

Only laughter. Tomorrow is a friend. A Chicago team *can* keep a promise.

Mission accomplished.

Say it was only a football game. Say it was *the* football game. It was more.

It was redemption, it was vindication, it was a great civic aspirin.

All the years, all the wait, all the alibis. Gone.

Stomped into the lint of the Superdome, stuffed into the three-cornered hat of a Yankee imposter that drew the short straw in the Super Bowl, way down yonder, down on the levee, the day Chicago lived.

Woof. Woof.

That's the sound of Bears, of these Bears, growling into quarterbacks, smothering ball carriers, making dreams real. The Monsters, no longer just of the Midway, but of America.

On one cruelly delicious afternoon along the Mississippi, the Bears made Chicago's generations the same, no longer separated by then, laced together by now, sharing one memory, a nearly perfect season, a nearly perfect Super Bowl.

The long night is over. Chicago's finger rises higher than its nose. Big shoulders wear new clothes. The wardrobe of champions. A toddlin' town can strut.

The happiest reward awaits.

Envy.

So long the special property of Chicagoans, jealousy must find a new address. Elsewhere apologies can be made. Up in New England, down in Miami, out in Los Angeles.

The world can watch Chicago grin.

The Bears made history and enemies.

The Bears will not be loved for their brutal mugging of the Patriots, not by the networks, who may have lost an audience by halftime, nor by anyone with compassion for the Patriots, those sad sacrifices, reduced to trying to win with a one-legged quarterback and an accidental coach.

The innocent Patriots, so used to gifts, found only torture, from Richard Dent and Mike Singletary and Jim McMahon and Willie Gault.

From people not even Chicagoans knew existed, Reggie Phillips and Jim Morrissey and Henry Waechter.

The rout was so thorough that the least menacing of all the Bears was the greatest, Walter Payton.

There were so many Bears terrorizing from so many places and so often, nothing New England had ever done deserved what happened to it.

Pity is theirs, and welcome to it.

Bears are now genuine bullies. Swaggering, bragging, backing it up.

McMahon, the punk quarterback, so insolent, so inspired, delivered for the Bears and for the cameras.

He ran out of headbands before the Bears ran out of ways to score—kicks, runs, interceptions, safeties, appliances.

Gault, the sprinter, redeemed a suspicious career. Doubt can now be carried off by the handles.

Matt Suhey ran, and someone remembered his name. William Perry scored and almost passed, adding another odd twist to his legend by giving more sacks than he got.

Dent was everywhere, choosing his victims along the Patriots' offensive line until he could find one who could block him. None could.

Singletary seemed to fall on every ball Dent dislodged from a Patriot. Mike Richardson was perpetually sticking a hand between the ball and the next available Patriot. Dan Hampton and Otis Wilson and Wilber Marshall were in the Patriot backfield so often they might have taken handoffs.

Dent was anointed the Most Valuable Player, an award that had to go to somebody on the defense since coaches are not eligible. Defensive coach Buddy Ryan should have gotten the prize, a car, or the whole defensive crew a Winnebago.

Ryan got a ride on the shoulders of his pupils, as did Mike Ditka, though Ryan's lasted longer.

Ditka. None of it would be possible without Ditka. He demanded only that his players give him their best, but only he is allowed to judge what their best is.

This was their best, as he knew it could be.

Ditka remembered the city he symbolizes and the old coach he refuses to forget. George Halas was there in Ditka's heart when he accepted the trophy, and Chicago was on his mind, all the patient Grabowskis by whatever name.

The Bears did not just break the curse of Chicago, they demolished it. Packed it off into a secret trunk that never needs to be opened again.

If only all those points the Bears didn't need could be borrowed by the Cubs, the Sox, the Hawks, the Bulls.

But if they can't, the example is there.

During those raw Octobers, when pennants are being measured for others, in those tardy springs when someone else's mercenaries soar higher or skate faster, it will be remembered that there was a day when a Chicago team said yes.

This is not an end but a beginning.

Super Bowl XX.

That's one.

Otis Wilson and Mike Singletary are pleased with the work of the '46' defense. (Tribune photo by Bob Langer)

Dan Hampton and Otis Wilson celebrate after sacking New England's Steve Grogan, who can only sit and watch. (Tribune photo by Bob Langer)

The Fridge blasts over the left side for a TD. (Tribune photo by Bob Langer)

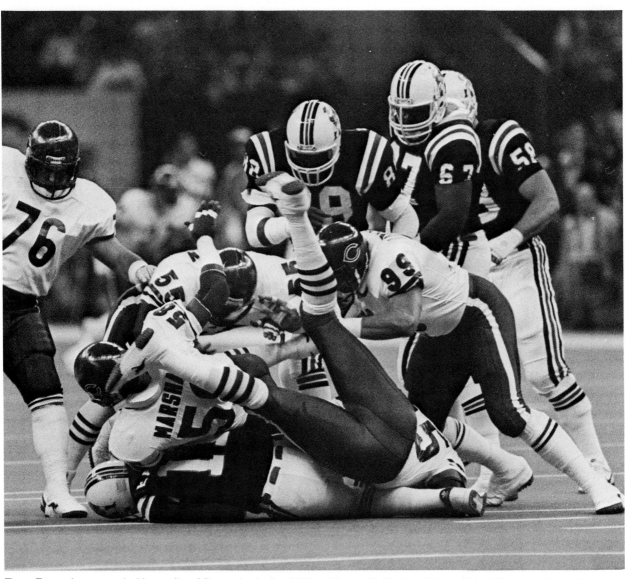

Tony Eason is pummeled by a pile of Bears, including Wilber Marshall, Richard Dent, Otis Wilson and Dan Hampton. (Tribune photo by Bob Langer)

Walter Payton gives Jim McMahon a Bear hug from behind as the team watches the clock wind down. (Tribune photo by Bob Wagner)

Dave Duerson leaps high to block Steve Grogan's view—but not the ball. (Tribune photo by Bob Langer)

Walter Payton shouts encouragement to his teammates. (Tribune photo by Bob Wagner)

Cold hands, warm hearts welcome Bears

By Ann Marie Lipinski
and Jerry Thornton

A thank-you note written on 10 tons of ticker tape was hand-delivered to the Bears who returned to sweet home Chicago Monday, Jan. 27, packing pride and a silver souvenir from New Orleans.

Five hundred thousand fans, hoarse from days of revelry, shouted hosannas as a caravan of cars and buses carried Bears players and management through the streets of the city's financial district. Gratitude rained down in the form of shredded canceled checks, Yellow Pages, tissue paper and computer printouts.

"Today, in this country, everyone is a Bears fan," screamed team president Michael McCaskey as he hefted the gleaming Vince Lombardi Super Bowl trophy from the podium at Daley Plaza. "*We* are the Super Bowl champs . . . *Woof, woof, woof, woof!*"

The fans returned the now famous trademark of the Bears defense.

Along the parade route, which began at Jackson Boulevard and LaSalle Street and ended at the plaza, temporarily named Bears Plaza, businessmen with briefcases, construction workers with hard hats, lawyers in fur coats, students with backpacks and mothers with strollers withstood a windchill of 25 below zero to serve as hosts in the city's welcome-home party.

"I may have to have my toes amputated but I've got to see this parade," said Wendy Rosiak, who traveled to the Loop from the Far Southeast Side Hegewisch neighborhood. "I've been a Bear fan since the day I was born."

Some diehard fans faced the frost and then asked for more.

"Papa, Papa, please let it snow!" said Tom Webb, as he looked heavenward for a sign of Papa Bear George Halas. "We want *Bears weather!*" Webb, a truck driver for the city, said he phoned his bosses Monday morning to tell them he wouldn't be in, explaining that the parade was more important than his paycheck.

"My biggest wish is that Mayor Daley were here to see this," Webb said. "Wouldn't he be a happy man? Oooooo!"

But celebration turned to some consternation when fans, many of whom had been waiting outdoors to see the players since early Monday morning, realized many of the Bears had gone into hibernation.

Eight of the Bears biggest stars—Jim McMahon, Mike Singletary, Jimbo Covert, Otis Wilson, Dan Hampton, Richard Dent, Dave Duerson and Jay Hilgenberg—had caught an early-morning flight from New Orleans to Honolulu for the Pro Bowl. Walter Payton had flown to Chicago earlier on a private jet and left for Hawaii, where Pro Bowl players were obligated to report Monday even if their team had won the Super Bowl.

But even those Bears who returned to Chicago were difficult to see. The team was shuttled through in buses with tinted windows too dark to allow the fans any visibility. The exception was Coach Mike Ditka, who rode through in an open limousine.

As the buses waded through the crowds and confetti in an effort to reach the plaza, fans mounted the vehicles and formed roof-top cheering squads. Others had pulled open the doors to the baggage compartments and climbed inside. Police barricades that had been set up to allow the players a clean path to the plaza podium were reduced by the city's celebrants to a pile of broken lumber.

In the end, only five of the players made it through the throngs and up to the podium.

"We had no idea the crowd would be that huge," said Ken Valdiserri, the Bears' director of public relations. "There were so many people, there was no way to get everyone on the stage."

Before Mayor Harold Washington told the fans, "The rest of the players can't get off the bus; you all get home safely," Willie Gault, Emery Moorehead, Steve McMichael, Tom Thayer and Kevin Butler, the place kicker who set a National Football League record this season for most points scored by a rookie, took the microphone.

"Isn't this sweet?" asked Butler. "Just make your plans for Pasadena [the California site of the 1987 Super Bowl] because we'll be stopping there next year."

Gault, who wore white, said simply, "Thank you, Chicago."

Fans climbed to rooftops, tree tops, light poles, canopies and the top of the Picasso statue to better their glimpse of the ticker-tape parade, a rowdy and romantic celebration which Chicagoans have bestowed on Charles Lindbergh, Franklin Roosevelt, Gen. Douglas MacArthur, V-J Day and the Apollo 11 astronauts.

"One of my fondest memories is from 1945 when my mother brought me to a ticker-tape parade at State and Madison for V-J Day," said George Tolbert, the manager of a Hinsdale securities firm, who sat on a LaSalle Street curb. "There was dancing in the streets, and the crowd was huge, but I've got to tell you that this is a bigger shoot-up."

Tolbert was accompanied by his wife and a friend, Tyke Ramm, who told the employees of his La Grange brick company that he would be out making business calls Monday. "And just to be on the safe side I turned off my beeper," Ramm said.

All along LaSalle Street, office workers formed human window displays, many of them sipping champagne and beer in an understandable suspension of workplace rules against alcohol consumption. Those whose windows were not painted or locked shut in a tribute to modern heating and cooling systems threw out once-important office documents in a steady hail.

"There's absolutely no work being done," said Chris Clancy of Milton Black & Associates on the 24th floor of 33 N. LaSalle St. where office workers had spent much of the day shredding phone books to throw.

One worker on the balcony of the City Hall–County Building attempted to read the shredded papers and joked, "Look, it says something about Clarence McClain."

Chicago police tactical officer Jerry Masterson looked up, blinking, to see the stream of papers flying from office windows and observed, "As long as they don't start throwing their typewriters, we're in good shape."

But, alas, not everyone on the streets Monday had come to celebrate.

"Excuse me. Can I get to work please?" pleaded Daniel Murray, a stock broker who had been trying for 10 minutes to make his way from the Chicago Board of Trade building to his office across the street. "Can I *please* get to work?"

The answer was a resounding no.

Also contributing to this report were Manuel Galvan, William Rectenwald, Don Terry, Cheryl Duvall and Rudolph Unger.

Mike Ditka rides off the field on the shoulders of Steve McMichael (unseen) and William Perry. (Tribune photo by Charles Cherney)

Dennis Gentry and Calvin Thomas celebrate the Bears' victory. (Tribune photo by Bob Langer)

Brian Cabral holds the championship trophy aloft in the dressing room after the Bears' victory. (Tribune photo by Bob Langer)

Bears' president Mike McCaskey hoists the Lombardi Trophy and Tom Thayer reminds everyone who's No. 1 at the team's homecoming. (Tribune photo by Frank Hanes)

Bears' fans welcomed the Super Bowl champions back to Chicago. (Tribune photo)

Fans swarm the buses carrying the Chicago Bears in a ticker-tape parade through chilly Chicago streets. (Tribune photo by Anne Cusack)

1985–86 Chicago Bears

NO.	NAME	POS.	HT.	WT.	AGE	NFL EXP.	COLLEGE
4	Steve Fuller	QB	6-4	195	28	7	Clemson
6	Kevin Butler	K	6-1	204	23	R	Georgia
8	Maury Buford	P	6-1	191	25	4	Texas Tech
9	Jim McMahon	QB	6-1	190	26	4	BYU
18	Mike Tomczak	QB	6-1	195	23	R	Ohio State
20	Thomas Sanders	RB	5-11	203	23	R	Texas A & M
21	Leslie Frazier	CB	6-0	187	26	5	Alcorn State
22	Dave Duerson	S	6-1	203	25	3	Notre Dame
23	Shaun Gayle	CB	5-11	193	23	2	Ohio State
26	Matt Suhey	FB	5-11	216	27	6	Penn State
27	Mike Richardson	CB	6-0	188	24	3	Arizona State
29	Dennis Gentry	RB	5-8	181	26	4	Baylor
31	Ken Taylor	CB	6-1	185	22	R	Oregon State
33	Calvin Thomas	FB	5-11	245	25	4	Illinois
34	Walter Payton	RB	5-10	202	31	11	Jackson State
45	Gary Fencik	S	6-1	196	31	10	Yale
48	Reggie Phillips	DB	5-10	170	25	R	Southern Methodist
50	Mike Singletary	LB	6-0	228	27	5	Baylor
51	Jim Morrissey	LB	6-3	215	23	R	Michigan State
52	Cliff Thrift	LB	6-1	230	29	7	E. Central Oklahoma
55	Otis Wilson	LB	6-2	232	28	6	Louisville
57	Tom Thayer	G/C	6-4	261	24	R	Notre Dame
58	Wilber Marshall	LB	6-1	225	23	2	Florida
59	Ron Rivera	LB	6-3	239	23	2	California
60	Tom Andrews	C	6-4	267	24	2	Louisville
62	Mark Bortz	G	6-6	269	24	3	Iowa
63	Jay Hilgenberg	C	6-3	258	26	5	Iowa
70	Henry Waechter	DT	6-5	275	26	4	Nebraska
71	Andy Frederick	T	6-6	265	31	9	New Mexico
72	William Perry	DT	6-2	308	23	R	Clemson
73	Mike Hartenstine	DE	6-3	254	32	11	Penn State
74	Jim Covert	T	6-4	271	25	3	Pittsburgh
75	Stefan Humphries	G	6-3	263	23	2	Michigan
76	Steve McMichael	DT	6-2	260	28	6	Texas
78	Keith Van Horne	T	6-6	280	28	5	USC
80	Tim Wrightman	TE	6-3	237	25	R	UCLA
82	Ken Margerum	WR	6-0	180	27	4	Stanford
83	Willie Gault	WR	6-1	183	25	3	Tennessee
85	Dennis McKinnon	WR	6-1	185	24	3	Florida State
86	Brad Anderson	WR	6-2	198	24	2	Arizona
87	Emery Moorehead	TE	6-2	220	31	9	Colorado
89	Keith Ortego	WR	6-0	180	22	R	McNeese State
95	Richard Dent	DE	6-5	263	25	3	Tennessee State
98	Tyrone Keys	DE	6-7	267	26	3	Mississippi State
99	Dan Hampton	DT	6-5	267	28	7	Arkansas

CHICAGO COACHES

HEAD COACH—Mike Ditka (4th Year)
ASSISTANTS—Jim Dooley, Dale Haupt, Ed Hughes, Steve Kazor, Jim LaRue, Ted Plumb, Johnny Roland, Buddy Ryan, Dick Stanfel

Ditka—the coach hates to lose

By Don Pierson

Mike Ditka laces conversations with disclaimers such as, "I don't know if that's good or bad," or, "I don't know if it's right or wrong."

He only knows how he feels. Sometimes, even he is not sure he likes it.

"I don't condone everything I do," he says.

Take it or leave it. Good or bad. Right or wrong. Ditka does not apologize; he warns.

He practices the adage: "If you're a leader, lead. If you're a follower, follow. Everybody else get out of the way."

"I hate to lose," said Ditka. "When I was kid playing Little League baseball, boy I hated to lose. I cried. It just hurt my feelings to lose. I don't like to lose. I'm not proud of that, but I just don't like to lose.

"I don't know how it came up."

Neither do his parents, Charlotte and Mike Ditka of Aliquippa, Pa.

Mostly, they got out of the way.

"Give the credit where it's due," said his dad. "First to him and second to his mother. I would like to say I was out there and caught ball with him seven or eight hours a day, but that was a rarity."

Instead, when the elder Ditka wasn't working on the railroad, toiling in the Jones and Laughlin steel mill or tending to union affairs, he would watch his son play baseball.

One day, he witnessed a remarkable scene. Mike was catching and younger brother Ashton was pitching. Ashton walked "one, maybe two batters." Mike ordered a conference on the mound and the two switched positions. This worked until the shortstop made an error. Mike switched to shortstop.

"The manager told me after the game, 'Mr. Ditka, I don't believe this.' I said, 'Tell me something. I don't either,'" said Mr. Ditka.

"I was sitting in the stands

Bears' coach Mike Ditka saw plenty of things to like during a 15–1 regular season in 1985 and the NFL playoffs in January, 1986. (Tribune photo by Bob Langer)

tearing my hair out. Michael had a disposition that he always figured he wasn't supposed to lose. If he hit the ball, he drove it 20 miles. If he missed it, you figured you had a broken bat at home plate."

Ditka's mother recalls that Mike's uncle gave him a full football uniform when he was 4 years old.

"Maybe he thought he should win because he had the outfit," said Charlotte Ditka.

Hating to lose meant hating anyone else who didn't hate to lose.

"I really believe this: If you accept defeat, then you're going to be defeated a heckuva lot more than you're going to win," Ditka explained. "You can be gracious in defeat, but boy, I'll tell you what, you can be gracious on the outside, but you better be doing flipflops inside. If you're not churning and turning, you're going to go out and get your butt whipped next time out. That's all there is to it. You'll start accepting it.

"I'm not sure that isn't what happened with the Bears for a

while. They didn't like losing, but it seemed to be a way of life, so they accepted it. You find ways to blow games. You find a way to blow a last-minute game in Minnesota just because those sons of guns have purple uniforms on. That's bull. I don't believe in that."

For Ditka, hating to lose seems to be a stronger emotion than loving to win. It is more the attitude of an underdog than a bully.

"I was never a bully," he said.

George Halas was the only man in the world who would have hired Mike Ditka to coach his football team.

"No question about it," said Ditka. "Too many drawbacks. First of all, there's an NFL image you have to be and maintain and I probably wasn't it."

Halas gave him the chance. Minnesota coach Bud Grant said it proved that it is who you know and not what you know.

Ditka draws a parallel to his idea to use William "the Refrigerator" Perry as a running back. Defensive coordinator Buddy Ryan wasn't giving him a chance to play defensive tackle.

"The hilarious thing about this Perry thing is it's kind of busted the staid image in the NFL that all running backs are slender, 6 feet tall, between 185 and 215 and built. This has made a farce out of that," said Ditka.

"Every underdog in society relates to Perry."

The image of Ditka as tempestuous bully must leave room for Ditka the careful compromiser. Ditka strives for success not by crude compulsion so much as by compromise, not by brawn so much as by brain. Wisdom is one of the compensations of age.

"When you get down to it, Mike is smart," said Dallas general manager Tex Schramm. "A lot of people want to picture him just as the tough bully. But Mike has a lot of sensitivity and compassion. You know he's competitive, but he also has good sense when he lets himself have good sense."

The record shows that Ditka has demonstrated the good sense to compromise at every turn because he remains uncompromising in his desire to win.

"If you have a goal and it's important enough to you, you won't let anything deter you from that ultimate big picture," said Ditka. "The big picture is winning and winning championships."

"I don't think he's an underdog," said his wife, Diana. "He is very confident in everything he does. But maybe he's trying to prove things to himself."

At football camp before his sophomore year, the 135-pound Ditka was kicked off a practice field by Aliquippa coach Carl Aschman for his own protection.

"I cleaned the latrines for the rest of camp. Never got back into another practice," said Ditka.

His mother asked Aschman why he was always picking on her scrawny son and Aschman told her it was because he thought he would be good. Aschman talked Ditka out of quitting before his junior year and Ditka dedicated himself to excellence.

"If he did push-ups, you could hear the house rock upstairs. He did it all himself," said his dad.

The grandson of Ukrainian immigrants, Ditka was encouraged by his dad to pursue sports as a way to get to college and away from the mills.

At Pitt, Ditka was "not as big a name as some of the other guys. I think that's where I understood that the harder you work, the more you get out of life. I became a pretty good football player, not because I was faster or could catch the ball better, but I taught myself to do a lot of things that other guys didn't.

"Everything was competitive. My whole life was based on beating the other guy, being better, being equal to, or just showing I could be as good as anybody else. I don't know if that's good or bad."

He begged his position coach, Ernie Hefferle, to let him practice against teammates instead of blocking sleds.

"When he walked on the field, Lord have mercy, everybody was his enemy," said Hefferle.

Teammate Chuck Reinhold could have sworn Ditka was bullying him at halftime of a Michigan State game when he bounced him off a locker.

Reinhold had missed a tackle against Herb Adderley to enable Michigan State to take a 7–0 lead.

Ditka doesn't recall beating Reinhold up, but he remembers confronting him: "We were coming into the locker room and he said: 'Well, we're only down 7–0. It's only halftime.' I said: 'Seven–nothing? That's bull. It doesn't matter what we're down. You had a chance to make a play and you didn't make it.'

"It was probably wrong to say it, but that's what I confronted him with. I'm sure I hurt his feelings and I'm not saying I was right. I apologized to him the next week. We were 4–3–3 that year. We were 17 points from being undefeated. But it's not important? What's important is what's important."

In Ditka's first game as a pro, the Bears were being embarrassed by Minnesota in the Vikings' first game as a franchise. Ditka told veteran guard Ted Karras to get the lead out of his rear end.

"He took a swing at me," said Ditka. "I was a rookie playing my first game. I wasn't supposed to say anything, but that never stopped me from saying things anyway."

Injured and nearly washed up when Tom Landry and the Cowboys called in 1969, Ditka worked himself into "the best shape of my life" to salvage his playing career.

Ditka's intensity inspired Landry to ask him to coach. Then, Landry threatened to fire him if he didn't learn to hang onto his clipboard.

Denver coach Dan Reeves, a former Dallas teammate, recalled an early encounter with Ditka in a card game.

"He picked up his chair and threw it. All four legs stuck in the wall," said Reeves. "I said, 'Man, this guy hates to lose.' "

"Sure, he's changed," said Landry. "You have to mature into the position or you have to get out of it."

Landry used to label Ditka "a Bear" because of his basic approach to strategy.

"I'm not fancy," Ditka said.

He took the shiniest team in the NFL to Irving, Tex., but Ditka doesn't want to be confused with "America's Team," the slick Cowboys.

This is "Chicago's Team." To Ditka, it always will be "Halas's Team," appreciated in "Brooklyn, Pittsburgh, Scranton, Wilkes-Barre, Birmingham, good work areas where people know what it's all about. We wouldn't fit too well in Beverly Hills, Miami, places like that."

When Halas answered Ditka's own letter of recommendation in 1981, Ditka had to live with a general manager, Jim Finks, who didn't hire him and with a defensive staff he didn't hire.

"It was the first compromise he made," said the Bears' current general manager, Jerry Vainisi. "But in his own mind, when he went out on the field, it was still going to be done his way. I think he tried to bull through all that and force it."

In his second game, a 10–0 loss to New Orleans that Ditka called the most humiliating experience of his life, he threw a tantrum that convinced him that "some of the players thought I was nuts, I'm sure."

Fortunately, a players' strike gave Ditka an eight-game cooling off period, and he began to realize that he couldn't control everything—and didn't have to.

"For the first time, you began to see a change in him," said Vainisi.

Ditka does not have the power to draft and trade players that Don Shula and Bill Walsh have, but he has flourished in a system that requires group compromise.

"He's a joy to work with," said director of player personnel Bill Tobin. "He's not afraid to listen."

Tobin is overjoyed because Ditka has put the right players on the field and weeded out the wrong ones. When he decided an untested ex-defensive tackle named Mark Bortz should replace veteran Noah Jackson at left guard, everybody feared that Bortz never would be able to handle players like the Cowboys' Randy White as well as Jackson could. It turned out that Bortz handles just about everyone.

When Halas died in 1983, Ditka had to learn to live with grandson Michael McCaskey, who did not decide to renew

Ditka's contract until after the '84 season.

"I didn't have anybody in my corner except Jerry Vainisi," said Ditka. "Everybody else had the magnifying glass out and they were looking hard."

Club president McCaskey said he wanted to sit down after the season and make sure he and Ditka agreed on the philosophies and principles of running a team in the 1980s on a budget that is not unlimited.

"I found that we both share a respect for what a lot of people call old-fashioned values. That work, effort, character, and heart mean as much as anything else," said McCaskey.

McCaskey said he was impressed by Ditka's willingness to learn from mistakes, his ability to innovate, and his decisiveness in making tough personnel decisions.

"Everybody knew he was a motivator," said McCaskey. "The question was always raised about his football smarts. This is a savvy and clever football coach who will do the smart thing."

After getting to the 1985 NFC title game and creating great expectations for the 1985–86 season, Ditka lost two of his best players—Todd Bell and Al Harris, who held out for more money. Naturally, Ditka wanted them back, but he shed few tears.

"We're playing without people we couldn't play without if you listen to everyone, that we *could not* play without, and we're undefeated," he said. "Why? Because one or two people don't make it; 45 people make it."

Ditka lived with what was left, including an insolent quarterback who makes Ditka's eyes cross at the mention of his name. Jim McMahon's irreverent attitude and uncompromising dislike of losing remind Ditka of himself. Ditka's ultimate compromise is that he has to put up with a player who is his clone.

Ditka likes to call plays, and McMahon sees that they can't always work. When McMahon changes them or audibles out of them, the results have been from good to spectacular. Sometimes, it is difficult to tell exactly how much this pleases Ditka.

"If people want to say we play good offense because of

Mike Ditka: "If you're a leader, lead. If you're a follower, follow. Everybody else get out of the way." (Tribune photo)

McMahon and Walter Payton, that's fine. I don't care. If they say we play good on defense because it's Buddy's defense, that's okay," said Ditka. "They're all working for the Bears. I don't want the credit. I just want the wins."

Players still think Ditka is often unnecessarily nuts on the sideline. But his sincere desire to win has transcended the histrionics. His players say they "understand" him even though they appreciate his Monday-through-Saturday style more than his Sunday game face.

Against the Lions Nov. 10, he screamed at Tim Wrightman when he thought the tight end had taken an improper split on a punting team.

"I said I had no idea what he was talking about," said Wrightman. "In the film the next day, he said, 'Tim, you were right.'

"He's not going to die of having a lot of stress built up inside."

At practice, Ditka rarely talks, let alone yells. He allows his coaches to coach. He has the power to fire any of his assistants, but he has made no changes, ruining his "my-way-or-not-at-all" reputation.

In a meeting room is where he makes the most sense to his players.

"What he's really great at is

he's a great motivator," said middle linebacker Mike Singletary.

"There's no question when I stand up and talk, a lot of guys say, 'Here we go again,'" said Ditka. "If they think they get themselves up, let them think it. It's better than not thinking it."

Whether or not they think it, they play hard. Ditka's legacy will be that his teams played hard.

"They play hard because I think they know they have to play hard to stay on the field," said Ditka. "There's nobody I wouldn't replace."

Chuck Mather, a former Bears' assistant coach and a former high school coach at Massillon, Ohio, pointed out that motivation is more important at the professional level than it is in high school or college.

"You don't have to dwell on it in high school or college like you have to in the pros," said Mather. "The great motivators are the ones who have won, whether they did it with fear or respect. In pro ball, 80 percent of winning is motivation."

Mather remembered an incident in 1965 when Bears' rookie Gale Sayers was being questioned by teammates and coaches alike about his toughness.

"Mike was one of his worst critics," said Mather. "Then against San Francisco, he made one of the greatest runs you've ever seen. I remember Mike jumping off the bench to run onto the field and pat him on the back. From that moment on, I always thought Gale got tougher. I think it had a lot to do with Gale Sayers being a great player."

The minute after the Bears survived their slugfest against the Packers in Green Bay Nov. 3, Ditka confronted linebacker Otis Wilson for committing a potentially costly personal foul late in the six-point victory.

"I jumped on Otis first thing. I don't give a darn we won," said Ditka. "We're not going to win a game in a situation like this if it happens again against a better football team. I don't care whose feelings are hurt. And Otis apologized."

Halas would be proud, of course.

"He hired me for two reasons," said Ditka. "First, he

wanted to hire his guy, not someone somebody else hired. And he believed I'd be tough enough not to take any bull. From players or anybody. The other things, he probably didn't even know if they'd work out."

Halas wanted to hire a Bear.

"You have to be one before you really feel it. If they cut Landry open, stars would fall out. I'm a Bear," said Ditka, who actually looks like a Bear and acts like a Bear, sometimes teddy, sometimes grizzly.

"I'll tell you something," said his dad. "I've seen him when he was very pleasant company. You couldn't ask for better. I've seen him when things weren't going right, and I'll tell you what, he wasn't fit to talk to."

When the Cowboys were beating the Bears at Soldier Field in 1984, a fan behind the bench asked whether Ditka was still on Landry's payroll. Ditka was incensed and exchanged profanities with the fan. He admits he hears such things and they hurt.

"I would almost like to get the Bears to a situation where nobody could say anything bad about them," said Ditka.

"The gratifying thing about all this is when people ask me what it means," said Ditka. "It means one thing: I've repaid a confidence."

Though he doesn't smile on the sideline, coach Mike Ditka manages a grin as he gets a pat on the back from a fan after his Bears pasted the Atlanta Falcons 36–0 on Nov. 24 in Soldier Field. (Tribune photo by Charles Cherney)

Winning mystique—nobody knows real McMahon

By Phil Hersh

What does it all add up to, this combination of simulated Charles Bronson, simulated Sid Vicious, simulated James Dean and simulated Ward Cleaver?

Where is it that he came from, this athlete with such a cosmic comprehension of his sport that he must have played in another place, presumably on another planet, before he landed here? Through the looking glass to that wonderland, is there a man of many dimensions or an Alice made 10 feet tall, with one dimension skewed by trick mirrors?

Why is it he can be rude, crude and lewd and have it pooh-poohed, even in polite society?

When was it that he got this distaste for losing, a man who has almost never lost, yet becomes intemperate about even the thought of it?

Who is this Jim McMahon, a character—what a *character*, chuckle, chuckle—or a series of characters? Is he simply role-playing with the cameras and the good times rolling?

"Nobody knows what I'm like," McMahon says, "and that's the way I want it. I want to keep them guessing."

Is it an act? Is he an actor? Does it make a difference?

We want our sports heroes to let their actions speak louder than words, yet are oddly uncomfortable if those actions fall outside conventional ethics. We want them to be like Homeric heroes, whose predetermined essence governs their existence, leaving us no surprise. We want them to be complete conceptions, not something in the process of being. It is hard to understand a piece of work in progress.

And Jim McMahon is nothing, if not a piece of work.

Quarterback Jim McMahon's season included a bizarre haircut and a fine for wearing an unauthorized headband, but it also included a 56.9 completion percentage and 15 TD passes.
(Tribune photo by Charles Cherney)

A television reporter approaches the quarterback in the locker room at Soldier Field. With lights on and camera rolling, he asks McMahon what he has done to pass the time on the sidelines. With a wild-eyed look, the quarterback holds up a copy of a skin magazine that makes Penthouse look like National Geographic.

"McMahon is the only person in the world who can honestly say, 'I don't care what other people think about me, I'm going to enjoy life and do what I want,' " says Dan Plater, McMahon's best friend and former teammate, both at Brigham Young University and briefly with the Bears.

"If people remember me as a good person, I'll be happy," McMahon says. "And if they don't, I'll be happy, because you can't please everybody."

Unless, that is, they are all children, whose demands are so much simpler. Invite McMahon into a roomful of kids, and they will immediately be crawling all over him or playing catch with him or getting his autograph. "My little kids could tell he had a big heart," says orthopedic surgeon Brent Pratley of Provo, Utah, whose words were echoed by a dozen others.

"The only time I've ever seen him open up is with children," said Carl Severe, in whose house McMahon lived during his last months at Brigham Young. "He doesn't relate well to adults."

A friend recalled watching McMahon lovingly exhort a 4-year old boy to eat his vegetables. And yet he needs no urging to behave like the eggplant that ate Chicago.

McMahon's wife, Nancy, once said to her husband, "Your kids will think you were a real weirdo."

"No," he answered, "they're going to think I was a cool dad."

One who butted heads with his teammates—and authority. One who dangled from hotel balconies hundreds of feet above the ground. One who wore sunglasses under his helmet at practice. One who let the nation watch him take a pain-killing shot on the sidelines. One who turned a bad haircut into a shaved head and then a prickly subject people talked about for weeks. One whose locker stall at Halas Hall in Lake Forest was recently decorated with pictures of his young children, Ashley and Sean, and a picture of an unidentified female breast. One who, as a child himself, was often unusually cruel to other children.

"I don't think those things are strange," he says, barely half an hour after he has explained some of those actions by saying, "I like to do strange things to see what they write about. I just like to act crazy to see what reaction I get. I laugh at myself, too, for some of the things I do."

And then when they write

about it, the headstrong McMahon calls them "idiots and puppets." Only a few weeks before that outburst on a paid radio appearance, he had sat through an unpaid, lengthy interview with a combination of diffidence and courtesy, filtering his words through a mixture of beer and chewing tobacco that turned into a viscous scum when he spat it into a paper cup.

"I get a big kick out of it all," he says. "People think they have the inside story, but I'm not the person they read about or see on TV."

"Jim wants an identity not only from football," says Ernie Jacklin, his high school football coach in Utah. "He wants people to know he's an individual. I don't think it's a bit phony."

McMahon's image may have been etched in stone by his actions in and around a nationally televised Thursday night game against Minnesota Sept. 19. He spent the Sunday and Monday nights before the game in traction with muscle spasms in his back. He missed practice Tuesday and Wednesday and developed an odd leg infection Wednesday. That was enough for Mike Ditka not to let McMahon start the game, even if the quarterback hadn't infuriated the head coach by spending part of one practice talking in the stands with ABC-TV analyst Joe Namath. Some time that week, McMahon had a meeting with Ditka that was more a shouting match, with papers flying around the coach's office.

McMahon kept making his point loudly on the sidelines in Minneapolis, letting Ditka know he was ready to play. Ditka finally put him into the game in the third quarter with the Bears trailing 17–9. In the next seven minutes, the essence of McMahon came out: All the fearlessness, defiance, surpassing talent and catalytic leadership ability were on display, as if this were the microcosmic look that would make the big picture clear.

Here was McMahon in the act of self-definition. Here was a man improvising his part in a script that seemed less the work of Ditka than of Sartre. Said one of Sartre's characters in the play "No Exit": "Only actions determine intentions."

Says McMahon: "I knew what was going on, and I knew what the game plan was, and I knew what I was supposed to do, and I proved it to them that night."

His first play, called as a screen pass, turned into a 70-yard TD bomb to wide receiver Willie Gault. His second play was also a TD pass; so was his eighth. None of the touchdowns looked remotely like anything in the playbook. The Bears won 33–24. McMahon slicked some goo into his 'do and went back into the hospital Friday for more rest.

What he had really put to bed was the modern image of a quarterback as a robot who comes to work with computer printouts and the Wall Street Journal. Open McMahon's briefcase, and all anyone will usually find is a sandwich. What would you expect from a man presumed to be out to lunch all the time?

"When I see him on TV, I say, 'Shoot, Jim, stop putting on a show.' That's not really him," says Norm Chow, BYU's receivers coach. "But it must be him because it has gone on so long."

"At 7 months, I began to become a brat," McMahon said in an autobiography written for English class his senior year in high school.

It wasn't long before his athletic ability became equally evident. When McMahon's mother, tired of chasing her 2-year-old *enfant terrible* through the house, tried to stop him from tormenting his brothers by throwing little balls at him, McMahon frustrated her by catching the balls.

"When he was 2, I'd have him outside with a broomstick handle as a bat, pitching rubber balls to him, and Jimmy would hit the ball all the time," says his father, Jim, Sr.

The confluence of talent and temper produced a remarkable athlete with a willful streak barely below the surface. And he was soon getting under everyone's skin.

Wrote McMahon in the section of his autobiography called "Zero to Five":

"The first few years of my life were trying times for my mother and others around me, but they seemed to handle it pretty well.

If they only knew what was in store for them in the years to come."

Jim McMahon was born Aug. 21, 1959, in Jersey City, the second of six children of Roberta and Jim McMahon. His parents—mother a Californian, father from Jersey City—met when they were on military duty at the 5th Army Machine Records Unit on Pershing Road in Chicago. When Jim was 3 years old, the family moved to California, staying with his maternal grandmother in Fresno until his father found a job as an accountant in San Jose.

The McMahons lived in a bungalow in an ethnically and racially mixed, lower middle-class neighborhood in San Jose within walking distance of their childrens' elementary, junior high and high schools. That was convenient for his mother because "I was in school as much as Jimmy was...He was always in trouble." Constant rounds of recrimination and apology with school officials led them to a child psychologist, who determined McMahon was hyperactive.

McMahon, a quick learner, was soon bored with school, and his idle mind turned to mayhem. He crawled under tables and poked classmates with straight pins lifted from the teacher's desk. He threw blocks and puzzles at the other children during rest periods. He became peevish with classmates who were slower in school and was, in his own words, "the neighborhood bully." McMahon was especially fond of picking on a chubby Hawaiian boy, and he threw rocks at a little girl on crutches.

"All I ever wanted to do was recess," he says.

Recess meant sports, where McMahon needn't wait for his classmates because he could simply play with the older kids. In an area of California loaded with talented young athletes, McMahon was a 9-year-old starter on football and baseball teams dominated by 11- and 12-year-olds. He was one of two sophomores in 30 years to start at quarterback for Andrew Hill High School in San Jose.

His problems were with elders. Told by his mother he had to wear a belt and tuck in his shirt for elementary school, McMahon would pull off his belt and pull out his shirt when he was still close enough to home that she could see it. Slapped by a 7th-grade teacher, he slapped her back in the face. Called for a net violation in a 9th-grade volleyball game, he cursed both the referee and a teacher who tried to calm him down. Told by a college coach to run a short pass off a three-step drop, he dropped back three steps, stopped, then kept dropping back to throw the long pass he wanted. For a touchdown, of course.

"The kids loved his overall cockiness," says Rick Alves, coach and guidance counselor at Andrew Hill. "They like a guy who talks big and then can back it up. He'd do it, even if you thought he was nuts to try."

Perhaps that best explains the stunning series of injuries that began at age 6, when McMahon nearly lost an eye. He was trying to untie a shoelace with a fork, but the fork snagged and flew into his eye, damaging the retina. Surgery restored his vision to 20/200, where it remains. (Think of that irony: a quarterback who has limited sight in one eye and an almost visionary idea of the game.) The eye became extremely sensitive to light, leading McMahon to wear the sunglasses that became a trademark when he switched from a utilitarian style to the mirrored, wraparound shades he favors now.

The eye injury was merely the beginning. He severely cut a hand riding his bicycle. Sprained an ankle jumping off a fence on a shortcut to a friend's house the week before his first game at Roy [Utah] High School. Caught chicken pox while his leg was in a cast from knee surgery at Brigham Young. Broke his hand early in the '84 season. Ended 1984 after 10 games with a lacerated kidney—who ever heard of anyone getting a lacerated kidney?—that threatened his future as a professional athlete.

"McMahon does things for a thrill, but he knows where he is going. He isn't on some sort of suicide trip," says Plater, a second-year medical student at the University of Southern California whose own career was ended by a brain injury. "I just hope he

can quit on his own terms."

Where he is going is always the end zone; so much the better if it means running over a defensive tackle to get there. His goal, in no uncertain terms, is winning, which sometimes leaves doctors at a loss to explain the things McMahon has done to his body and which is why the Jan. 5, 1986 playoff game with the New York Giants was his first. The kidney injury kept him on the sidelines for the Bears' two playoff contests following the 1984 season.

"Football is not an easy game to play," McMahon says. "It's brutal, it's a sick game, but it's fun. My wife says she doesn't worry as much about me getting hurt as she does about me throwing an interception, because she knows that makes me angrier.

"No one wants to get hurt or walk away crippled, but I'm sure that will happen anyway. As long as I can walk out there, I will. When I came in, I wanted to last at least 15 years. Now I want to last week to week. But I don't think I'll quit. They'll have to drag me out of here."

That was apparent even as a sophomore in high school, when McMahon responded to aspersions about his guts by letting a witless assistant coach yank a dislocated shoulder back into place during a game. That macho folly obviously damaged the arm more, but it was only a minor annoyance until McMahon's junior year at Brigham Young, when he could barely lift it before a game at Hawaii. He played "on guts alone," according to Pratley, throwing 55 passes in a 34–7 BYU victory.

Bored after the game, McMahon decided to take the shortcut between his 24th-story room at a Waikiki hotel and the room a floor below where Plater, who calls himself "McMahon's better half," was studying the anatomy of a shark he had secreted in his luggage for the trip. The sore-armed quarterback simply hung from his balcony and dropped in to see Plater, who was less surprised than impressed by the way McMahon got there.

"You know how hard it is to do that?" Plater asks.

Like everyone else, Plater marveled at his friend's athletic

ability and daring on the road less traveled. Jack Germaine, head coach at Andrew Hill for three decades, watched in awe as McMahon ran a two-minute offense to win his first game as a sophomore quarterback. He only wished his time with McMahon didn't seem as short, because the quarterback and his family moved to Utah before his junior year of high school.

"I cried when he left," Germaine says. "It was like finding a huge nugget while you were panning for gold and then dropping it back in the water and seeing someone else find it."

The man who picked it up, Roy High School coach Jacklin, learned he had struck it rich from McMahon's father, who had come to Utah ahead of his family. Jacklin's team was already blessed with two senior quarterbacks, but he made one a linebacker and the other a defensive back after McMahon exceeded even his father's advance billing. The only regret Jacklin has is taking a year to switch from a wishbone to an I-formation offense.

"After you watched him throw the ball once, you knew Jim was good," Jacklin says. "He had the best release I've ever seen.

"What really set him apart was his ability to lead. He never was reluctant to take charge. His greatest ability was being able to make decisions quickly. Right from the start, he was calling nearly all the plays."

But major colleges weren't calling McMahon, a small kid—he is still just 6 feet tall and 190 pounds—from a state with only 26 schools in the enrollment class against which Roy competed. Notre Dame, his first choice, never showed the slightest interest. He wound up going just 80 miles down the road to Brigham Young, where he set so many passing and total offense records the NCAA needed a recount before it determined the total to be 70. Or was it 71?

They would have been even greater if he had not spent a year as a back-up, another splitting the starting job and a third as a redshirt. McMahon thought, with some justification, he was ready to play from the minute he put on a Brigham Young uniform, no matter that eventual

All-America Marc Wilson was the man ahead of him.

"The first time we met," Pratley says, "it was on the sideline at the first game of his freshman year, and I asked Jim what he did. He said, 'I'm a quarterback, but they've got this quarterback out there who can't do crap, and I should be playing.' Jim was the punter, too, and I bet him he couldn't kick the next one over 40 yards. It was raining cats and dogs, the ball was soaking wet and he kicked it 65 yards."

His end results, measured in wins and losses, were as impressive, just as they would be with the Bears. Despite having just a 3–4 record as a starter during a National Football League debut disrupted by the players' strike, McMahon was the highest-rated rookie passer in the league.

Now, three seasons later, he kicks butts and commands the respect of his teammates on the field, especially the linemen, with whom he feels such kinship that McMahon sponsors their weekly off-the-field revels. Whether the respect brings the winning, or the winning brings the respect, is as hard to answer as why losing leaves such a bad taste in the mouth of a man who rarely has to eat his confident words.

"How can he do it?" Plater is asked.

"Why does he beat you at dominoes or cards all the time?" Plater asks, unable to answer the question without asking others. "No one knows, except that he hates to lose and does the things *he* thinks are going to make the team win."

"You see a guy that plays as hard as he plays, and it inspires you to do your job," says Bears' center Jay Hilgenberg. "You know if you do, he'll make things happen."

The linemen admire McMahon for that and his defiance and his fearlessness—or, if you will, recklessness. The quarterback never shuns a challenge, whether it is blocking a linebacker or disregarding the silly play some coach sent in from the sideline, where he couldn't possibly know what was happening on the field. McMahon rolls up his shirt sleeves, quite literally, and gets down to the dirty work.

"Kids would follow him to the

ends of the earth," says Glen Tuckett, the Brigham Young athletic director.

"Jim's idiosyncrasies pose absolutely no problem to anyone on the team," says Bears' safety Gary Fencik. "What Jim has is a gunslinger attitude—risk-oriented, not afraid to take chances. He is quicker on the draw because he has presence and vision."

It is the vision granted the Gretzkys and the Birds and the Peles, who have such a clear point of view they understand the way their games work. "He sees a picture the way a photographic shutter does," says BYU offensive coordinator Roger French. "One click, and it's recorded in his mind."

One click is all McMahon usually gave it. He didn't watch much film even at Brigham Young, finding such exercises as boring as school work. What was the point, if you had the answer right the first time?

"It's hard for some people to realize, but he can look at film once and get what he needs," says BYU head coach LaVell Edwards. "He would come out to practice and yell at the prep team for not lining up exactly the way they were supposed to to mimic the opponents' defenses.

"He's not big, he's not whatever else, he's supposed to have impaired sight, but the guy's got the greatest sense and vision of anyone on the field. It's like a sixth sense."

What McMahon lacked was a sense of where he was off the field. Or maybe he knew exactly where he was, but didn't have the common sense to roll with the punches instead of throwing them. Whatever, records became the least celebrated of the things he broke at BYU.

"Jim has adventure written all over his face," Tuckett says.

On a fall afternoon in Provo, there was a small sign on the door of the Brigham Young fieldhouse. "ATTN: FOOTBALL," began the notice, designed to remind the players of their obligations to the school's grooming code if they wanted to receive their monthly room-and-board stipend:

"Don't be surprised
"If your check is denied
"Because your hair needs a

clip
"Or we can't see your lip
"Just come looking clean
"And you'll get all the green
"Pay day Friday."

The sign was accompanied by an illustration of a spike-haired outcast who bore a clear resemblance to comedian Martin Short and . . . Jim McMahon.

"Jim thrived on being different at BYU," Plater says.

The prevailing wisdom now is that he was always in hairy situations because BYU is BYU, with its prohibitions against alcohol, tobacco and caffeine, not that McMahon is McMahon, with his predilection for substances forbidden to Mormons. Thus, the logic goes, his differences with the school's Office of Standards were magnified.

"Jim was not a real major problem here," Edwards insists. "He's brutally honest, and some of the things he says and does disappoint me a little, but Jim is Jim."

McMahon has said leaving Brigham Young was like getting out of prison. He has said he would never go back there to finish the work for his degree. "It's not the easiest place to get an education, when they're playing mind games with you all the time," he says. Asked if the school would be ashamed or proud of him, he answered, "Probably a toss-up."

Although McMahon resented being the occasional object of the proselytizing that is part of the Mormon commitment, he had no trouble committing to relationships with Mormons, on or off the field. He became so close to one, Plater, that McMahon provided most of the down payment for his friend's house in a fashionable Los Angeles suburb. And he married another, Nancy Daines, whom he calls "the most positive influence in my life." So what if he showed up to meet Nancy's Mormon parents with a beer in his hand and a chew in his mouth?

"Her parents accepted me for what I was, not what everyone wanted me to be," McMahon says. "She never liked dating Mormon guys because they were boring. She grew up in California, and she knew that people drink beer and chew tobacco. Mormons outside of Utah are pretty normal; Provo is like a big bubble."

McMahon was guilty of drinking a beer on a golf course, of an occasional smart answer to the campus cops who ticketed his rattletrap Dodge Charger for minor violations and of telling his coaches where they could stick the punting team they tried to send on the field with BYU behind by 20 points late in the 1980 Holiday Bowl. In the final 4:07, McMahon quarterbacked the Cougars to three touchdowns and a 46–45 victory in the game that, before Minnesota, established his reputation as the quintessential winner.

"Jim is a study in contrasts," Edwards says. "He's a real good family man, and then he paints this sort of thing."

When the Office of Standards decided McMahon's artwork looked more like spray-painted graffiti, it left Edwards to discipline his quarterback. Edwards accomplished that once by grabbing the quarterback by the facemask and pulling him to his knees. And yet the coach, too, kneels at the shrine of McMahon's ability.

"I'd sign a lifetime contract if I could keep a guy like him," Edwards says. "Jim is basically a good person."

It has been said that McMahon went to BYU because he confused it with BYO, which seems logical enough for a man who often lets "I drink therefore I am" stand as 100-proof evidence of his existence.

McMahon admits he went to Brigham Young for one reason: to play football at a school where the passing game was emphasized and the quarterback's role was paramount. That is also why he stayed, despite impatience at having to play behind Wilson for most of three seasons, in one of which McMahon was redshirted. His father, Pratley and Edwards all claim some credit in talking McMahon out of transferring, but the quarterback probably listened only to his own angry voice.

"I didn't want to let them win, to let them make me leave," he says. "I just wanted to show them. Once I was on the field, they couldn't do anything to me. They would have to wait until

after the game if they wanted to yell at me.

"After I redshirted, I said to Nancy, 'I'm going to break every one of those records the other guys [Wilson, Virgil Carter and Gifford Nielsen] set.' I got most of them."

Most of all, he got the education he wanted—or however little he needed—in the art of making the passing game work.

"Jim is a taker, an opportunist," Eleanor Olson, a Roy High School teacher, says. "He puts his needs above those of others, and his needs were to go to a school that would get him where he wanted to get.

"Jim would never wear a sign that said, 'I am Third,' like the title of Gale Sayers' book. Jim's would say, 'I am First.'"

Both of Jim McMahon's parents encouraged him to think and act like No. 1. "If you don't feel you're the best, no one else will believe in you," Roberta McMahon says.

That might be one of the few points of agreement between McMahon and his family, especially his mother. She is a strict disciplinarian and a Mormon. His father, a Catholic, was closer to Jim until they had a bitter disagreement over the choice of Jerry Argovitz as his original agent.

The relationship between Roberta McMahon and her son became strained early, when she insisted on his not being able to play sports if he didn't play by her rules about grades and general conduct. She had him temporarily removed from teams in both junior high school and high school and, after an offense she preferred not to pinpoint, had her husband drop Jim from the Little League team he was coaching.

"If I couldn't play baseball, I was going to be an ass," McMahon says.

As a teenager in San Jose, he threw bats and helmets. As a teenager in Roy, when his basketball coach asked McMahon to stop lifting weights for football or turn in his uniform, McMahon immediately grabbed the uniform and handed it to the coach. The result, not surprisingly, was the coach relented because he wanted the talented McMahon

on the team.

"Jim is the guy who can do it and get away with it," says Jacklin, who could only shake his head when McMahon stretched the meaning of a short pass to whatever distance he wanted.

As an adult, McMahon has thrown a table hockey game after Plater beat him. When golf beats him, as that game does almost everyone, he heaves the clubs. Or, if the spirit moves him, he brings a three-wood to its knees by bending it over his.

"When we first started playing golf together, the sound of the club was bigger than the sound of the ball, because he threw it," Pratley says. "When you play with McMahon, it sounds like helicopters: 'Whoop, whoop, whoop, whoop.' But I've never thought of him as a spoiled brat, just competitive as hell."

Ditka feels the same way about a quarterback with whom he has such a tenuous relationship that the coach has said "shut up" were the only words they exchanged in weeks. "I expect that to change for the better," says Bears' president Michael McCaskey, fully aware that getting one or the other to concede anything will be difficult.

Act your age, is how the expression goes. Act it, not be it, as if there is something of a put-on in being anything more than a child. At age 26, arguably one of the best men alive at his profession, Jim McMahon still can hear himself singing, "I don't want to grow up, I don't want to go to school."

McMahon says the only thing he wants to do after he retires is to own a golf course—a possible dream, given his five-year contract worth nearly $1 million a year—where the only rules would be his. "Yeah," says Plater, "and the first rule would be: 'Shoes and shirts, no service.'" McMahon wants to walk barefoot in the park, but with his luck, he'll step on a rusty nail.

"I want to go out and play where you can't be hassled by anybody," he says.

Not Mormons. Not mothers. Not coaches. Not by anyone who says Jim McMahon can't be Jim McMahon, whoever that is.

Less is more for Payton

By Don Pierson

Jim McMahon, the Bears' quarterback, was serious and sincere when he said it: "Walter Payton is still a big part of this offense."

It just sounded strange. For most of his first 10 pro seasons, Payton was the *only* part of the Bears' offense. "A big part" sounded little. It was sort of like saying water is still a big part of Niagara Falls.

McMahon was on target, as usual. Payton no longer carries the Bears on his shoulders. The team is strong enough to move around on its own. But Payton is still very much there, pushing, pulling, coaxing, pointing the way.

It is difficult to determine exactly how Payton feels about all this. His thoughts are often as elusive as his legs.

"A lot of people put a lot of emphasis on the running game or the passing game," Payton said. "But this Chicago Bear team does not consist of one individual. Or not even two individuals. Everyone has contributed in some way, shape, form or fashion."

Payton has been extremely cautious about what he says these days. To some, his manner has suggested a twinge of jealousy. To those who know him best, it suggests an anxiety that whatever he says will be misinterpreted.

"I've never been in this situation before, even in high school or college," he said. "I don't know the feeling I'm supposed to feel. Every game is pressing, and there is more pressure for next week. If that's what winning means, right now it feels pretty good.

". . . [Winning] doesn't mean you have to gain 100 yards each game. It doesn't mean you have to throw the ball for 400 yards each game."

Not until Oct. 13, 1985, when the Bears beat the 49ers, did a victory put Payton above .500 for the first time in his pro career.

Walter Payton has more carries and more yards than anyone else in history, and his team—after 11 seasons—has finally won more games than it has lost since he arrived in 1975. Is it any wonder he has trouble tackling his own feelings?

"I hear people say he's lost a step. That's pure bull," said fullback Matt Suhey. "He's absolutely as good as he's ever been. Probably, he is contributing as much as he ever has, but he doesn't have the ball doing it. He picks up blitzes, blocks as well for me or Calvin [Thomas], runs great pass patterns. Anything they're asking him to do, he does."

If anyone had any real doubt about Payton's place, it should have been erased in 7 minutes 33 seconds of the 49er game Oct. 13 when the Bears marched 66 yards for the clinching touchdown:

Payton left 9, Payton middle 4, Payton left 7, Payton middle 2, Payton middle 2, Payton left 6, Suhey left 2, Payton middle 3, Payton left 2, Suhey no gain, Suhey pass 9, Dennis Gentry middle 3, Payton left 17 and a TD.

"It's the mark of a very, very good football team when you can run the ball when they know you're going to run the ball," Suhey said of the first old-fashioned Bear drive this season.

"Walter thrived on what happened out there," said coach Mike Ditka. "That was more fun than anything else in the game."

"It's not that we haven't done it because we couldn't do it, but because teams have given us the opportunity to throw the ball and McMahon and the receivers have done a fantastic job," Suhey said.

The opportunity to throw has been around for 10 years, thanks to Payton. The ability to throw is a more recent development, no reflection on Payton.

"A couple years back, he felt if we were going to lose, he wanted the responsibility," Suhey said. "And you'd be crazy not to give it to him. But we have so many weapons now."

To the Bears, there is no problem delineating the leadership structure of the offense. To McMahon, "Payton is still the leader on this ballclub. Everybody knows we can count on Walter."

To defensive tackle Dan Hampton, Payton is "the real leader, but it's hard for the players to identify with him on a playing basis because he is the best running back and possibly the best football player of the last 50 years.

"Walter is the leader by example. McMahon is the guy they can associate with as one of their own. No one on this football team and no one in the NFL is actually in Walter Payton's league."

The Bears are just on his side.

"Right now, I'm just happy to be in this situation," Payton said. "To be with a team that for so long has struggled and tried a lot of different methods to get to a good situation, and now it's finally here. I just hope I can be a small part in making it stay there."

Walter Payton: No. 34 in the Bears scorecard and No. 1 in the hearts of the Chicago fans! (Tribune photo by Ed Wagner Jr.)

Walter Payton gives a Falcons' defender the slip. In his 11th pro season, he averaged almost 20 carries a game for the Bears. (Tribune photo by Charles Cherney)

Walter Payton has hurdled opponents' bodies throughout his career. After 11 seasons, "Sweetness" finally cleared a huge obstacle and made it to the Super Bowl. (Tribune photo by Ed Wagner Jr.)

Perry's story shapes up as a big family affair

By Phil Hersh

Maybe this belongs in Ripley's. Maybe it should have a big, black headline in one of the scandal sheets everyone skims in the supermarket checkout line.

It is a story few would dare put in a daily newspaper.

It is one that had to be kept in the deep freeze as long as William Perry was cooling his heels in South Carolina. If one word of this had leaked out, "the Refrigerator" might have seemed like nothing more than a picnic cooler.

Now it can be told.

I watched William Perry go seven hours without eating.

This happened in Aiken, S.C., over the Fourth of July weekend. From the time Perry met me at the Augusta, Ga., airport until the time I left him at his two-bedroom townhouse on the outskirts of Aiken, the Refrigerator never raided one.

Easy as pie, you say?

It would have been if all we had done was chew the fat in his living room. But we spent a couple hours at his mother's house, where Inez Perry's cooking had always been so good William says everything she made was his favorite dish.

"William wasn't choosy," Inez Perry says.

None of her 12 children could afford to be. They simply went through the four gallons of milk that were delivered every other day, ate cereal out of mixing bowls, and learned quickly what mama meant when she said "help yourself" to the cauldrons of food that rolled out of her tiny kitchen each day.

Says Daryl Perry, a 5-foot-11-inch, 220-pound defensive back at Gardner-Webb College and the smallest of the eight brothers:

"We would eat whatever Wil-

William Perry proves that "the Refrigerator" can catch TD passes, gingerly hauling in a 4-yarder in the 16–10 victory at Green Bay on Nov. 3. (Tribune photo by Jerry Tomaselli)

liam decided to leave us."

Now William Perry is beginning to understand what that was like. For the first time in his life, he has to leave the table hungry. No more of mama's cooking or the meals his wife, Sherry, used to make: breakfast of grits and cheese, eggs, bacon, toast and jelly; lunch of four sandwiches; and dinner of several pieces of chicken, peas, heavy biscuits, rice and gravy or macaroni and cheese.

Even before the Bears saw Perry collapse in the 90-degree temperatures at their Platteville, Wis., training camp, they had warned him to stay out of the kitchen. His college

coaches had said the same thing, but they lacked the Bears' ability to make Perry's pocketbook thinner.

"No one ever told me I *had* to go on a diet until I was drafted by the Bears," Perry says. "Nobody ever told me I had to lose weight when I was little."

The chances of doing that were slim, because he never was. Perry weighed 13½ pounds at birth and 50 pounds more than anyone else in his first-grade class. No one understands better than William Perry does the paradox of talking about when he was little.

"Even when I was little, I was big," he says.

Howwwwwwww big is he?

Size 61 sport jacket; triple-extra-large shirt; 23 neck; 48 waist.

"But I need pants with a bigger waist to get around my thighs," Perry says. No wonder: Each thigh is 34 inches around.

"I just gain weight faster than the average person," he says.

He has not had to custom-order clothes for his 6-3, 330-pound body. Perry just walks into Belk's department store in Aiken, or Anderson-Little in Greenville, S.C., and buys them off the rack.

"There's some big guys down here," he says.

Many of them are his brothers. Freddy, age 32 and still a feared semipro football player, goes 325 pounds. Michael, the 19-year-old baby of the family who is called "Little P," is 6-2 and 285.

Perry's 60-year-old father, Hollie, is only 5-11½ and 200 pounds. "The size comes from my wife," he says. Inez Perry, who has sturdy legs and the bow-legged gait of the fine athlete she used to be, is 5-9½. Her daughters are big enough they never had to worry about being pushed around by their brothers.

"How could we pick on them?" asks Michael, a sophomore linebacker at Clemson. "They'd beat our behinds."

"In that household," says Sherry Perry, "William's size is normal."

It was so daunting when William asked her to dance in junior high that she told him to go away because he was too big. He persisted, but when they started dating at Aiken High School, her family and friends wondered what she was doing with such a giant.

"I stopped thinking of William as big," she says. "I just started thinking of him as muscle-built. If William was to see someone as big as he was with a lot of fat, not muscle, he would laugh and say, 'I wouldn't let myself get that big.'"

Call that seeing the big picture, the way Clemson defensive lineman Ray Brown did when he squeezed into an elevator with Perry three years ago.

"He nearly took up the whole elevator," Brown says. "I called him GE because he was as big as a refrigerator."

When the Bears made Perry their No. 1 draft choice in May 1985, they insisted on a contract with tons of weight clauses and didn't think it was so funny when Perry showed up in training camp larger than life, after a two-week holdout over his contract.

In their immediate attempts to cut William Perry down to size, some Bears said things that reduced him to chopped liver. Defensive coordinator Buddy Ryan called him "a wasted draft choice and a waste of money." Head coach Mike Ditka, being more polite about a draft choice he helped to make, said Perry had a long way to go.

The criticism of his physical condition, however justified, belittled some considerable achievements. Perry was a consensus All-America as a Clemson junior and made three All-America first teams in 1984, when he set Atlantic Coast Conference records for sacks and tackles for loss, and school records for causing and recovering fumbles.

"William could go hard maybe five plays in a row, but he could make plays when you'd think he'd be loafing," says Steve Berlin, who played next to Perry in Clemson's defensive line.

"Against Wake Forest, he ran down a back 25 yards downfield. That's not bad for 350 pounds."

A three-play sequence against North Carolina last year is an even better illustration of what Perry can do in short bursts. On first down, he hit all-ACC running back Ethan Horton for a 1-yard loss; on second down, he hit Horton for a 5-yard loss; on third down, he rushed the quarterback into an interception.

"I was the best nose guard in the country, and the Bears knew that when they drafted me," Perry says.

The problem is how much better the Bears—and Clemson—thought Perry could be if he had worked harder at staying in shape. At one point, he would have had a hard time bench-pressing himself because the weight he was carrying (390) came dangerously close to what he could lift (438) on infrequent visits to the weight room.

"People who only saw him play at 350 and 370 pounds don't know what kind of player William can be," Berlin says. "He doesn't have to lift a weight, and he can lift a house."

Says Don Telle, Clemson's assistant strength coach: "We all knew if he trained, 500 pounds [bench-press] would be a joke. We were talking about 600 pounds for him. In the back of my mind, I thought of William as an Olympic lifter because he is so explosive and so quick."

That quickness is surprising to everybody. Telle remembers the first time he saw Perry do "wave" drills, which demand that players shift their movement from one direction to another at the sound of a whistle. "He was like a cat," Telle says. "He would run over everyone else because he could change direction so fast."

Perry says he can dunk a basketball, although he declined an invitation to demonstrate that. Berlin says Perry can throw a football 70 yards and kick a 50-yard field goal.

"And you should see him swim and dive," Berlin says. "The man can do flips off the high board. You know how walruses are, clumsy out of water and then graceful when they get in. That's what William looks like."

William Perry developed his wide range of athletic skills at the recreation center across from his parents' house. The location was a blessing for Inez Perry because it meant she could tell the kids to get out of the house and not worry about where they were going.

The Perrys' six-room house a couple blocks from the Aiken city jail is less tumbledown than tired from its two decades of trying to hold the Perrys. With one bedroom for the boys and one for the girls, there wasn't much room for roughhousing, and Inez Perry made that clear.

"The most problem I had was with them flopping in chairs," she says. "We'd be replacing chairs all the time.

"I told them if they wanted to rassle, they had to hit the door. They knew I didn't like fighting or people to mistreat each other. If they passed the first angry word, I would pass the second and third."

Inez Perry, who works as a cook and dietitian at Aiken Prep, has elegant high cheekbones, an accent that seems more New York than South Carolina and a pervasive sense of calm. Sitting in a living room cramped with trophies, fanning herself with a picture of two sons, she maintains the bearing of one who has endured.

This family of titans knew she was a rival as fearsome as Zeus. Whether she was chasing them back toward home with a flyswatter or applying the strap if they didn't move fast enough, it was not difficult for the children to size up the situation. The only person William Perry needed to fear was his mother.

"There wasn't no trouble for us to get into," he says. "We were either going to school or playing or eating, one of the three."

That was all Inez Perry wanted. She was able to keep her kids from getting hungry for other excitement.

"William wasn't no hard child to manage," she says. "You tell him something, and William would do it. He would go around the neighborhood asking to rake yards, and everyone wanted William to rake theirs."

William often shared his raking business with Michael, then pooled their profits to buy cookies or cakes. "We'd buy about 100 cookies, and he would give me five," Michael says, with a shrug.

There was simply no way to stop William Perry from having his cake and eating it, too. Neighborhood kids were often afraid to play with him because of his size. After letting William fool around with the Aiken Prep basketball team, the team's coach told Inez, "I put five guys on him, and they couldn't hold him down."

"People always wanted me on their side in basketball because I can set a good pick," William says. "It takes a long time to get around me."

William Perry has no problems making light of his size. As a Clemson junior, he posed for a publicity fold-out in which refrigerator doors that said "GE Clemsonaire Model 66" opened to show Perry in the icebox holding two bags of groceries. As a senior, he did a life-size poster that still serves as wallpaper for rec rooms and newspaper offices throughout the country.

"I never get uptight when people talk about my weight or how big I am," he says. "I've got a sense of humor, and I'll go along with them as long as they've got a sense of humor."

What he once thought was fun-ny almost drove Sherry away. In high school, she tired of watching William and his friends bully people and make jokes at others' expense. They broke up for nearly a year.

"William was real loud, very demanding and pushy," she says. "He would pick people up and swing them around. Then he kind of changed. He got more mature and started taking things serious."

"I had to mature," he says. "I thought I was going to lose her. I stopped joking around with the guys and taking more of a stand of my own."

The only time Sherry still worries about William's size is when he plays with their 2-year-old daughter, Latavia. Even though the child is as big as most 5-year-olds and packs a wallop when she beats on her daddy's 54-inch-chest, Sherry cringes at their horseplay.

"He plays with Tay Tay so rough I sometimes think he's going to kill her," Sherry says. "I tell him, 'William, you don't know how heavy your hand is.'"

"I love to hit people . . ." William says. "That's what I like about defense. An offensive tackle gets a good lick on a guy every now and then, but it's not too exciting to play offense. On defense, you can let yourself go.

"I like having a direct hit on somebody. It feels good."

Ask William Perry to recall the hits he remembers most, and he is confused.

"There were so many," he says. "I can go on and on."

The one best remembered at Clemson came in the Wake Forest game in 1984. Perry hit the blocker in front of Wake Forest's punter so hard the man was knocked into the air, where he blocked his own team's punt. Perry picked up the loose ball and returned it 36 yards to set up a touchdown.

That is the kind of return the Bears want on their reported $1.3 million investment in William Perry. They hope that making nearly 25 percent of that four-year contract contingent on physical condition will give him food for thought. His family, at least, is sure the Bears haven't bitten off more than they can chew.

"I think he can be All-Pro," Michael Perry says. "If William puts his mind to it, he can do anything."

After all, believe it or not, William Perry went seven hours without food.

William Perry proved he could do more than run with the football after playing his way into the starting defensive lineup at tackle. Here he sacks Vikings quarterback Tommy Kramer. (Tribune photo by Ed Wagner Jr.)

Revived Bears scorch Bucs

By Don Pierson

The Bears had half a notion not to show up for their season opener Sept. 8.

Soldier Field felt more like a steam iron than a gridiron, so it was a Sunday afternoon better suited for relaxing in the shade.

After the Bears' defense and special teams finally joined Jim McMahon and Walter Payton for the festivities, things turned out more than halfway decent. They beat the Tampa Bay Buccaneers 38–28 to surprise 57,828 fans, who suspected defensive holdouts Todd Bell and Al Harris were working the scoreboard by telephone during the first half when the Bucs led 21–7 and 28–17.

"I was kinda disappointed the fans got on our butt," said McMahon, who was making his first regular-season appearance since Nov. 4, 1984, when a kidney injury nearly ended his career.

"We got down two TDs, and we started hearing the boos again. Hey, we can come back and score."

Had the fans forgotten?

"I was asking Walter when the last time was we were really down and able to come back," said safety Gary Fencik. "He mentioned the Kansas City game in 1977."

Payton's memory is as sharp as his footwork. Indeed, the Bears came from being down 17–0 on Nov. 13, 1977 to beat the Chiefs 28–27.

When the Bears saw thermometers on the plastic turf that registered 133 degrees, they got the hint that this wasn't going to be another no-sweat encounter with the Bucs.

The football players from Florida felt at home until they looked up and realized they never had scored 28 points in a first half in their lives. They thought the game was over.

The Bears, behind 28–17, felt more hot air from coach Mike Ditka and defensive coordinator Buddy Ryan during intermission.

Two plays into the third quarter, defensive end Richard Dent leaped like a cheerleader and tipped a pass from Tampa Bay quarterback Steve DeBerg into the arms of cornerback Leslie Frazier, who returned it 29 yards for an easy touchdown.

"I was thinking interception because they ran the play in the first half and he threw behind the receiver," said Frazier. "If he had thrown to the receiver, I felt I could have intercepted it."

Frazier was playing in a three-deep zone in perfect position for an interception even without the tip.

"You look for one thing to trigger you," said Ditka. "It shocked me when I saw it. It was the one pump we needed."

The Bucs still had a 28–24 lead and James Wilder, who had gained 105 yards in the first half. But the Bears had made some adjustments.

"We started tackling him," said linebacker Otis Wilson.

After Frazier's interception return, the Bucs made only one first down in their next three possessions. It was an 11-yard run by Wilder, and Dent answered it by sacking DeBerg for 13 yards.

A punt set up the Bears at their 38, and McMahon was at his best.

He hit four passes in five attempts, including a crucial 15-yarder to flanker Dennis McKinnon on third and 4 from the 40.

On third and 6 from the 9, McMahon rolled right and fired a bullet pass to fullback Matt Suhey in the corner of the end zone. The Bears had their first lead, 31–28 with 27 seconds left in the third quarter.

It was a play designed for man-to-man coverage, and the Bucs were in a zone.

"Matt kept weaving back and forth, and when the linebacker turned his head, that's when I threw it," said McMahon.

Suhey made an outstanding catch and a great effort to keep both feet inbounds.

It was Suhey's only catch on a day when McMahon used eight receivers and completed a career-high 23 of 34 passes.

He still had time to hand off 17 times to Payton, give to other runners 13 times and keep it 4 times, and the perfect balance—34 passes, 34 runs—helped Payton gain 120 yards, his 64th 100-yard game.

"Perfect game plan," said Payton. "And we stuck with it."

The Bears averaged 6½ yards on first down, enough to control any defense.

"We knew our offense could come back," said Wilson. "Tampa doesn't have the good defense everybody kind of says they do."

After the Bears took the lead, Tampa Bay coach Leeman Bennett stuck with his game plan, but Wilder lost one yard in his next three carries, and Frank Garcia lined up to punt. Bears' rusher Shaun Gayle noticed a new blocker on his side.

"I dipped my shoulder and went right past him," said Gayle. "Usually, you can do something a couple times until a guy catches on. But they had someone new."

Gayle blocked the punt, and the Bears had the ball at the 13. McMahon hit Calvin Thomas for 12 yards and leisurely rolled out to cover the final yard for his

GAME 1

second touchdown to make it 38–28.

The Bucs got three more first downs on one drive, but Wilson forced Wilder into middle linebacker Mike Singletary for a loss of a yard on third and one at the Bears' 20. Donald Igwebuike hit the upright on a field-goal attempt, and it was over.

"A championship defense makes plays when it has to make them," said Ditka.

The Bucs made only 4 of their 17 first downs in the second half and only 95 of their 307 yards. Wilder got only 61 of his 166 yards after the half.

The Bucs scored first on a long drive featuring Wilder and wide-open receivers.

"I didn't recognize the Bear defense," said Fencik. "And it had nothing to do with Todd or Al. Everybody was not playing well, and Tampa did a very good job of preparing."

When McMahon came back with a 21-yard touchdown pass to McKinnon, the Bucs came back in half a minute with a 58-yard kickoff return by Phil Freeman and a 44-yard touchdown pass to Kevin House.

The 21–7 lead came after a Tampa Bay punt bounced back-

wards into unsuspecting Bears' return man Ken Taylor and was recovered at the Chicago 11.

After the Bears closed to 21–17 with 2:35 left in the half, the Bucs drove 77 yards and Wilder scored.

"Our defense was not asleep," said Ditka. "Tampa is a good team."

The defense begged to differ.

"We thought we played terrible," said cornerback Mike Richardson.

By giving up 307 yards, the Bears' defense will not be ranked No. 1 in the league for the first week since 1983.

Jim McMahon looks for someone to spike the football for him after scoring against Tampa Bay in the season opener. (Tribune photo by Ed Wagner Jr.)

Pats easy, but stars are ailing

By Don Pierson

Jim McMahon's back and Walter Payton's ribs were tender before the Bears' Sept. 15 game against the New England Patriots.

Afterwards, they hurt only when the Chicago players were laughing about their 20–7 victory against a team that wasn't ready for back-breaking, rib-rocking defensive football.

If the Bears didn't have to line up Thursday, Sept. 19, against the Vikings in Minnesota in an early NFC Central Division showdown, McMahon and Payton might have been able to hug each other.

Instead, McMahon was looking forward to a night in traction "or something to get rid of this." Payton was looking forward to three days without people wrapping their arms around him.

Both players expressed confidence that they will be ready. But neither had previously expressed fear about his condition. Neither showed up on the Bears' injury report.

Coach Mike Ditka expressed more hope than confidence.

"I think Jim will be fine," said Ditka. "I think Walter will be hurting for another week. If we can get through the Thursday, he'll have time to rest. If they can't play, somebody else will have to strap it up and go."

McMahon said he "slept wrong" last Monday night and thought sessions with a chiropractor had straightened him out.

"It's not my neck that's hurting; I think it's a pinched nerve in my back. It started messing with my delivery," said McMahon.

Payton had taken a hit against the Buccaneers in the season opener.

"It was doing good during the week, but to get a direct shot onto it right on the same spot, it's ironic," said Payton. "There's nothing broken or out of place. It's just so badly bruised it really hurts to move."

The Bears needed them for only a little while against New England.

Payton reinjured himself on his first carry of the game, a 6-yard gain. Big plays on first and second downs kept the Bears out of passing situations and away from Patriots' pass rushers Andre Tippett and Don Blackmon all day.

McMahon took a jolt in the first quarter, but he already had passed to flanker Dennis McKinnon for a 32-yard touchdown on the fifth play to stake the Bears to a 7–0 lead that was insurmountable.

The play was almost identical to the first touchdown against the Buccaneers in the opening game.

"Last guy we'd ever hit on that pass," said Ditka. "Jim finds people."

He was looking for tight end Emery Moorehead, but McMahon doesn't think it's unusual to go to a third or fourth alternate.

"Dennis just beat his man," explained McMahon.

"Without that drive, we would have been in for a heckuva day," said Ditka.

McMahon played for the next two quarters, and Payton was in and out while the Bears painstakingly stretched their lead to 20–0. Then the quarterback and the runner sat out the final quarter.

With 9:03 left, the Bears lost their shutout when Patriots' quarterback Tony Eason found running back Craig James isolat-ed on Bears' linebacker Wilber Marshall. He lofted a short pass over Marshall's head that James turned into a 90-yard touchdown, longest in New England and Soldier Field history.

Until then, the Patriots had crossed midfield for only one measly play. They got to the Bear 49 with 16 seconds left in the half and enjoyed it for exactly four seconds until Bears' middle linebacker Mike Singletary sacked Eason for 8 yards. It was the second of three sacks by Singletary, who also returned an interception 23 yards to set up the Bears' final points.

"Singletary was great as usual," said Ditka. "He moved a couple guys right into holes where the play was coming, and they stuffed it."

Payton gained only 39 yards in 11 carries, but it was 12 yards more than the entire Patriot rushing attack managed.

Eason ducked for his life and was sacked six times, completing only 15 of 35 passes and throwing three interceptions for the first time in his short pro career.

"They were predictable," said Bears' strong safety Dave Duerson. "Every week, we put three games into the computer and they were just so heavily typed. If they kept doing what they were doing for the three previous weeks, they were going to play into our hands."

Sure enough, Patriots' coach Raymond Berry did not disappoint Bears' defensive coordinator Buddy Ryan.

"No surprises," said Duerson.

"They ran right into our hands 95 percent of the time. We had a game plan of 150 pages, and they ran right into it."

They didn't run very hard, either.

"Their receivers are patsies,"

GAME 2

said Duerson, recoining a phrase that has described the Patriots forever. "They were very easy to bump and run."

While the defense was repaying the offense for favors of Sept. 8 against Tampa Bay, the offense controlled the clock, passed effectively and won without much help from Payton. With the Patriots overplaying the run, the Bears got 10 first downs by passing, only 7 by running.

McKinnon caught all his 5 passes for 73 yards in the first half as the Bears took a 10–0 lead

and blew two other opportunities when Payton fumbled and McMahon threw an interception on a flea-flicker.

A 21-yard field goal by Kevin Butler came with 37 seconds left in the half after an option pass by Payton was incomplete. It was one of four trick plays Ditka called.

Until the fourth quarter, the Bears faced only one situation when it was worse than third down and five. On the other hand, the Bears were able to convert only five of 16 third-down

plays and were especially ineffective near the goal line.

The Bears got their second touchdown after Willie Gault caught a 43-yard pass to set up a 1-yard plunge by fullback Matt Suhey.

"Any way we can win is good for us," said Ditka. "You see the mighty are getting their butts knocked off. There are a lot of heirs to the throne. We don't pretend to be one of the people on the throne, but we think we have a right to take a shot at it."

Dennis McKinnon catches a pass against New England during their Sept. 15 regular-season meeting. The Bears won at Soldier Field, 20–7. (Tribune photo by Bob Langer)

McMahon's magic saves Bears

By Don Pierson

Jim McMahon talked his way into the game and played his way into America's football consciousness on Thursday, Sept. 19, in one of the most dramatic quarterback performances in Bears' history.

McMahon threw three touchdown passes in seven throws in the third quarter to lead the Bears to a 33–24 comeback victory over the Minnesota Vikings, who had a pretty good quarterback themselves in Tommy Kramer.

With his back aching and his right leg infected, an angry McMahon convinced coach Mike Ditka to let him replace Steve Fuller with 7 minutes 22 seconds left in the third period and the Bears trailing 17–9.

First play: 70-yard touchdown pass to Willie Gault.

An interception by linebacker Wilber Marshall five plays later gave McMahon the ball on the Vikings' 25.

Second play: 25-yard touchdown pass to Dennis McKinnon.

"After the first two plays, I told him, 'Third time's the charm,'" said Walter Payton.

The Bears got the ball back on a punt and McMahon completed two of four passes before hitting McKinnon for a 43-yard touchdown.

In the span of 6:40, McMahon had completed five of seven passes for three touchdowns.

"I must have been blessed," McMahon said. "I can't remember the last time I threw three TDs like that."

Most amazing was that none of the touchdown passes was planned.

"The first play I almost fell on my face. I felt like a fool and thought, 'What a start,'"

McMahon said. "It was a blitz, and luckily Willie was looking, so I threw it up. It was supposed to be a screen pass to Matt Suhey."

The second and third scores were versions of the same crossing patterns that McMahon and McKinnon turned into touchdowns in the first two games against Tampa Bay and New England.

"The receivers said they were open downfield, so when I got in there, I was looking downfield," said McMahon.

McMahon had not started because he had not practiced and Ditka said he feared risking further injury.

"I don't know how you write scripts for the kind of game you saw out there," said Ditka, who turned and shook his head in disbelief on the sidelines after McMahon's third touchdown pass.

Gault finished with 6 catches for 146 yards, while McKinnon had 4 receptions for 133 yards.

The whole thing even tickled the sore ribs of Payton, who struggled his way for 62 yards on 15 carries and said he never had seen anything like McMahon's performance.

"It was like one of those Notre Dame old-time movies," said Payton.

The victory put the undefeated Bears in sole possession of first place in the National Football Conference's Central Division, which threw a new and modern image onto an unsuspecting public.

"This was an AFC West game," said safety Gary Fencik.

Kramer completed 28 of 55 passes for 436 yards and 3 touchdowns against the proud Bears' defense, which finally sacked him 4 times and intercepted 3 of his passes.

"He's got eyes in the back of his head," said Bears' defensive coordinator Buddy Ryan.

But McMahon turned the nationally televised show into his own private showcase. He finished with 8 completions in 15 attempts for 236 yards and a renewed image as a miracle worker.

"I haven't played on national television for so long I wanted to show my friends I could still play," McMahon said.

"I was praying he was coming in," said McKinnon. "He is known to have miracles happen."

McMahon had not practiced all week because of a mysterious kink in his back and an even more threatening infection in his right leg.

"Looks like gangrene to me," McMahon said.

The leg flared up the day before the game. McMahon said doctors told him it was the result of an open wound on the back of his passing hand that has not healed.

McMahon spent Tuesday afternoon sitting in the bleachers at the Bears' Lake Forest practice site chatting with his idol, ABC-TV commentator Joe Namath, while his teammates worked.

"That's why I wanted to play. He was doing a thing on me at halftime about me keeping healthy, and here I was sitting down. I was glad to get in and show him I could still play," McMahon said.

Fuller completed 13 of 18 passes for 124 yards, but the Bears managed to score only on three of Kevin Butler's four field goals with Fuller at the helm. They had the ball in Viking territory seven straight times under Fuller, but sacks and a costly interception in the end zone had

GAME3

them behind 10–9.

Kramer was magically eluding the Bear pass rush and moving the Vikings downfield. When he hit wide receiver Anthony Carter for the first of his two touchdown catches, the Vikings were ahead 17–9 and Ditka turned to McMahon.

"I got in his ear during warm-ups and told him I felt ready. I stayed in his ear at halftime and then after the first series of the third quarter, I said, 'Let me go, I'm ready,'" said McMahon.

"We just needed a spark. We were moving, but we just couldn't get it into the end zone."

Did the game plan change?

"I didn't see much of the game plan because I didn't practice."

Even after McMahon's third touchdown pass, Kramer wasn't through. He hit Carter for a 57-yard touchdown bomb to bring the Vikings within 6 points at 30–24 with 9:19 left in the game.

So McMahon struck again. After the referee had to stop the 30-second clock because of crowd noise, McMahon hit a streaking McKinnon down the sideline for 46 yards to quiet the place down.

An 18-yard scramble by McMahon set up a 31-yard field goal by Butler with 5:35 left that put Kramer more than a touchdown away.

McMahon had been angry all week about his physical condition and Ditka's insistence on seeing him practice before allowing him to play.

"I wasn't in a good mood," said McMahon. "I think the reason they didn't start me was they wanted to make sure I'd be healthy the rest of the year. That's what Mike told me before the game. I said: 'I'll be ready. Don't hesitate to use me.'"

Jim McMahon raises his fists as time winds down on the Bears' Super Bowl victory. (Tribune photo by Bob Wagner)

Gault takes off and Bears score

By Don Pierson

The Bears continue to grab fortune by the throat and shake it until it turns out to be good.

When Willie Gault took the opening kickoff from Washington Sept. 29, he handed off to linebacker Wilber Marshall on a reverse that backfired.

The next time, he lost the ball in the sun and it luckily bounced through the end zone for a touchback.

The third time, the Redskins must have been set up to ignore him. Gault's 99-yard kickoff return for a touchdown charmed 63,708 fans in Soldier Field and 44 Bear teammates who went on to smother the Redskins 45–10.

At the time of Gault's sprint, the Bears were losing 10–0. Rarely has a football game turned so suddenly. But this was a rare football game, and the Bears are a rare team, off to their best start (4–0) since their last National Football League championship year, 1963.

"I don't know what happened out there," said coach Mike Ditka. "We've tried to emphasize what a team can do—offense, defense and kicking team—and I think you saw the picture."

Gault's return started an avalanche of 31 points in the second period that was a Bear record for one quarter.

"The kickoff return turned on everybody, even the fans," said Ditka. "There were a couple curse words going through the audience before that."

Greatness is not measured in one-fourth of a season, but the Bears have won their games the way great teams win them. Somehow, they find a way.

They have come from behind in three of the four games. They have won when they have controlled the ball and when they haven't. They have won despite injuries and holdouts.

They have more than won; they have dominated. The Redskins are the defending NFC East Division champions. The Bears sent them home with a 1–3 record and their worst loss since a 53–0 pounding by the New York Giants in 1961.

In the Redskins game, the Bears won when Walter Payton was a blocking back and when Jim McMahon was a receiver and when Gault didn't catch a single pass.

They won when Redskins quarterback Joe Theismann was a punter with a lone boot of 1 yard.

They won when tackle Jimbo Covert and guard Kurt Becker sat out with injuries and were replaced by Andy Frederick and Tom Thayer. They won when strong safety Dave Duerson also sat out and was replaced by Shaun Gayle and in some defenses by Marshall.

They won when Payton gained only six yards in seven carries. It was his lowest total since the Redskins held him to five yards in 1981. That time, the Redskins won 24–7, when McMahon was a senior at Brigham Young and Joe Gibbs was an innovative young coach enjoying his first victory.

Times change. Football's all-time leading rusher finally has a team capable of carrying him on its shoulders in return for past favors.

The Bears won when McMahon called audibles out of running plays for his first two touchdown passes. McMahon also caught one from Payton during the 31-point blast.

McMahon started 0 for 4 with an interception and finished up 13 of 19 with 3 touchdowns. His last one was a 33-yarder to Payton that was Payton's first touchdown of the year.

The Bears scored five straight times in the second quarter on Gault's return, a 14-yard pass to flanker Dennis McKinnon, a 10-yard pass to tight end Emery Moorehead, a 13-yard pass from Payton to McMahon, and a 28-yard field goal by Kevin Butler.

After Gault's run, the scoring drives consumed 1 play, 3 plays, 5 plays and 7 plays.

On their first possession of the third quarter, McMahon needed 10 plays to drive 80 yards, the Bears' only drive of more than 36 yards. They closed out the scoring in the fourth quarter on a 1-yard run by Dennis Gentry after a 90-yard interception return by cornerback Mike Richardson.

"The kickoff was the biggest play of the game," said McMahon. "I had started out real bad, 0-for-4 and an interception. We heard the regular boos, but I think they're finally starting to realize the Bears can come back. We have the explosive players."

Gault's return virtually took the Redskins out of the game. Punter Jeff Hayes pulled a thigh muscle on the kick and didn't help it by chasing Gault.

"I saw blocks by Dennis Gentry and Shaun Gayle and a bunch of guys were on the ground," said Gault of his first pro kickoff return for a touchdown. "Real early, before I went through the hole, a guy almost stopped me."

At the 20, Gault burst through the hole. At the 45, he faked out Hayes. At the Washington 30, he cut inside Barry Wilburn and sprinted to the goal post. It took 19 seconds, almost twice as long as he used to do it in a track suit.

"Remember, I had to move a couple times, but I must be getting real slow," said Gault.

GAME4

54

"He was the catalyst up in Minnesota," said Ditka of Gault's 70-yard touchdown catch against the Vikings Sept. 19. "You've seen not only what Willie means to this football team, but the impact he's going to have on our league, because his speed is just exceptional. I marvel at what he does when he runs."

On the first Redskin play after Gault's run, linebacker Otis Wilson leaped over a blocker to nail George Rogers for a loss on the same play that Rogers had turned into earlier gains of 28 and 29 yards. After Theismann was sacked by defensive end Tyrone Keys, the Washington quarterback—substituting for injured Hayes—had to punt.

"They don't pay Joe Theismann to punt," said Ditka.

The ball traveled sideways 30 yards and forward 1 yard. The Bears took over at the Washington 14 and called a draw play.

"I saw we were in a blitz situation," said McMahon. "The free safety flew toward Willie and opened up the middle for Dennis."

McKinnon beat cornerback Vernon Dean for the touchdown.

Three plays later, Richard Dent rushed Theismann from the left side in the 46 defense and stripped him of the football.

Dan Hampton recovered the fumble at the 22. On third and 3 from the 10, a toss to Payton was called in the huddle. Again McMahon changed the play when he smelled a blitz. Payton nailed the blitzer, safety Tony Peters, and Moorehead ran alone to the flag for an easy touchdown.

Dent tackled Rogers for a 7-yard loss on the next play. The Redskins let back-up quarterback Jay Schroeder punt, and his first offering was for 22 yards, giving the Bears the ball at the Washington 36.

On third and 12 from the 13, Payton took a handoff on a Stat-ue of Liberty play and faked a run. He avoided defensive tackle Darryl Grant and threw back to McMahon.

McMahon had eluded end Dexter Manley, who had vowed harm to Payton and McMahon early in the week. No one followed McMahon into the end zone, where he made a diving catch.

"For two years, we've established that we can run the ball, and we look across the line of scrimmage and see eight guys there," said Ditka. "When McMahon gets that look, he's got the leeway to audible. It's just the way it's going to be."

McMahon said he called perhaps 10 audibles. Payton estimated maybe 6 were on runs called to him.

"You have to take advantage of it," said Payton.

"Walter mentioned on the sideline, 'If you see the blitz, just keep throwing the ball,'" said McMahon, who doesn't need much encouragement.

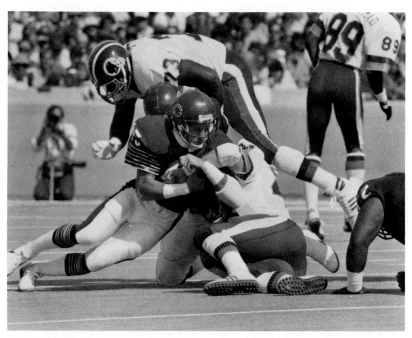

Gary Fencik picked off five passes to raise his career total to 35 and move within 2 of Bears' all-time leader Richie Petitbon. (Tribune photo by Ed Wagner Jr.)

Wilber Marshall (58) puts the big squeeze on Washington Redskins quarterback Joe Theismann and forces a fumble in the Bears' 45–10 rout on Sept. 29 at Soldier Field. (Tribune photo by Ed Wagner Jr.)

Guard Mark Bortz (62), shown here blocking Washington's Darryl Grant, was thought to be too slow to make it in the NFL, but he has become a steady performer in the Bears' offensive line. (Tribune photo by Charles Cherney)

'Bad' Bears just good enough

By Don Pierson

The Tampa Bay Buccaneers don't know any better, and the Bears don't know any worse. That's the main reason the Bears stayed undefeated Oct. 6 and the Bucs stayed winless by a score of 27–19.

The Bucs' only excuse is they failed to recognize the alternative. They had the Bears down 12–0 and figured that was right where they didn't want them.

For the fourth time in the first five games of 1985, the Bears came from more than a touchdown behind to win. Again, they were led by quarterback Jim McMahon, who this time also led them into the hole with his worst first half of the year.

"I was just kinda wandering around out there in the first half," said McMahon. "I don't know why. I just wasn't very sharp. Fundamentally, I was very bad."

It took three big catches by tight end Emery Moorehead and two touchdown runs by Walter Payton, the 100th and 101st touchdowns of his career, to put the Bucs away in the fourth quarter. The Bears hadn't led until Kevin Butler's 30-yard field goal put them up 13–12 on the final play of the third period.

"We were fortunate," said coach Mike Ditka.

"I don't think we were lucky," said McMahon. "We finally started executing. We knew we could come back and win. I don't feel lucky. We're a good football team."

To that, Ditka agreed, answering "Yep" when asked if he thought he would be 5–0 heading to San Francisco for an Oct. 13 rematch against the NFC champion 49ers.

"I believe in these guys," said Ditka, who was screaming his belief at them on the sidelines during most of their shaky performance.

McMahon and Ditka disagreed on how best to finish off the Bucs. McMahon won that argument when he talked Ditka into passing twice instead of running on the Bears' final touchdown drive.

The Bucs had closed to 20–19 on a 25-yard touchdown pass from Steve DeBerg to Gerald Carter with 5:21 left. It would have been 20–20 if they hadn't aborted an extra-point try in the first half with a wild snap.

The Bears had taken a 20–12 lead on Payton's 4-yard run with 7:51 to play, but the cushion wasn't enough because the defense was unable to get to DeBerg all day, and Buc receivers ran wide open.

The defense shut down running back James Wilder with only 29 yards in 18 carries. That's why the Bucs couldn't score any more than they did. But with 5:21 left, they were only one point behind.

It was third down and 3 for the Bears at their 24 with 4:01 left. Ditka called a run. The Bucs called time, and McMahon went to Ditka.

"I figured, heck, we had a good 3½ to 4 yards to go," said McMahon. "If we don't make that first down, they've got good field position, and who knows what would happen."

Moorehead had already caught seven passes for 106 yards for the biggest day by a Bears' tight end since Ditka. Two catches for 31 yards had kept the first Payton touchdown drive going.

The Bucs had shut down wide receivers Willie Gault and Dennis McKinnon, leaving Moorehead alone against linebackers.

"Most tight ends in the league can beat a linebacker," said McMahon. "Emery made tough catches. We've got to have those big plays."

McMahon wanted to throw a slant-out to him. "I knew we'd get three yards on that type of play," he said. Moorehead got 8.

"The old man came through," said Ditka of the nine-year veteran tight end.

"One of the biggest plays of the game," said McMahon.

It set up another big one. On second and 11 from the 41 at the 2-minute warning, Ditka called another run.

"I told him, 'Hey, they're going to be blitzing. Let's throw the ball,'" said McMahon. "He asked me which play I liked."

McMahon called a post pattern to Gault off a play-action fake.

"He just told me, 'If you can't get it, don't let them get it,'" said Gault.

Gault made a tumbling catch at the 11 for a 48-yard gain. McMahon was buried by blitzers. Two runs by Payton clinched it.

McMahon finished with 22 completions in 34 attempts after an 8-for-17 first half. He threw an interception in each half, first to set up the Bucs' first touchdown and second in the end zone on the Bears' opening drive of the third quarter.

"I wasn't up late," said McMahon, perhaps putting a finger on an excuse. "I just don't know what happened. I'm upset with my play. Everybody executed well except me in the first half. I made some stupid reads and didn't throw well at all.

"Foolish football on my part. I wasn't setting my feet. I knew what I was doing as soon as the ball left my hands. I'm my worst critic. I know when I screw up."

"It looked like he was rolling

GAME5

off his back foot, like he was going backwards," said Ditka.

The Bucs showed a defense that surprised the Bears, shifting nose guard David Logan into a gap and forcing the Bears' offensive line back to a drawing board.

"Mike said at the half, 'Hey, they're not beating us. We're beating ourselves,'" said tackle Jimbo Covert. "We kept plugging away, plugging away, plugging away."

The Bears drove 71 yards with the second-half kickoff before McMahon threw his second interception to safety David Greenwood. Payton had 20 yards after a first half of only 9.

"It was time for us to play ball," said Payton. "That drive was the boost we needed."

It was also strong safety Dave Duerson getting the interception back with a theft of his own at midfield.

Moorehead caught two passes for 32 yards, and McMahon finally threw a strike to McKinnon for a 21-yard TD to make it 12–10 with 3:40 left in the third period.

The Bucs answered with a fumbled snap from center that defensive tackle Steve McMichael recovered at the Tampa Bay 21, setting up Butler's go-ahead field goal.

The come-from-behind stuff might be getting familiar, but it's not getting comfortable.

"It's not good," said Ditka. "But if you can do it, I think it really helps your ball club."

Dispositions are another matter.

"I got a little carried away today," said Ditka. "We can't let down. Maybe I shouldn't jump on people like I do, but it's too important to let it slip by without mentioning it."

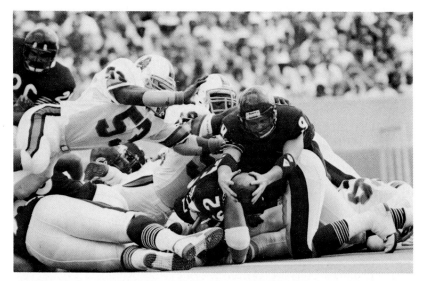

Jim McMahon, extending himself for a one-yard TD score against Tampa Bay, is a competitor in every sense of the word. (Tribune photo by Charles Cherney)

Mike Hartenstine puts pressure on Tampa Bay quarterback Steve DeBerg Oct. 6. The visiting Bears won 27–19 despite DeBerg's 346 yards passing. (Tribune photo by Ed Wagner Jr.)

Bears show 49ers who's boss

By Don Pierson

The Bears hailed the 49ers as the best and flailed them like all the rest on Oct. 13. By a score of 26–10, they staked their claim to the top of the National Football League.

"It's only for a week, but we're pretty good right now," said coach Mike Ditka, who had praised the world champion 49ers while plotting their burial.

It didn't totally make up for the Bears' 23–0 loss in the 1985 NFC title game and it won't help them in their next game Oct. 21 against the Packers in Soldier Field. But it made them feel awfully good for the moment, which they grabbed for all it was worth.

The Bears are a prime-time act, cantankerous and convincing, carrying the memories of elephants and an attitude to match.

They even unveiled their elephant backfield in the last seconds, letting 325-pound defensive tackle William Perry play fullback and carry the ball on the final two plays of the game.

"I just wanted to see if he could run with it," said Ditka.

"I was looking for the end zone," said Perry. "When the 49ers saw that I was the ball-carrier, their eyes got real big."

It was a 325-pound love letter to the 49ers and coach Bill Walsh, who had used 265-pound guard Guy McIntyre as a blocking back for a play or two in the 1985 NFC title game.

"Today was our day," said Ditka. "A great win for us. We beat a heckuva football team. We challenged them with our offensive and defensive lines. That's as good as we can play. The lines got the game balls."

Jim McMahon passed to a quick 16–0 lead and the defense squeezed the 49ers dry, holding them to 45 yards and only 3 first downs in the second half. To make certain they wouldn't stir in the final quarter, Walter Payton ran them down.

The 49ers had closed to 16–10 by halftime and were looking to make a move in the third quarter when the Bears ended it with a classic touchdown drive in the final quarter that was vintage Payton.

"Walter had fire in his eyes in the huddle," said flanker Ken Margerum.

"Everybody knows we can count on Walter," said McMahon. "He's still a big part of this offense."

Kevin Butler's fourth field goal made it 19–10 with 13:09 left in the game. He hit from 34, 38, 27, and 29 yards, two of them coming after 49er fumbles.

"I thought the kicking game would play a big role because you just don't pull out on the 49ers," said Butler.

With 11:14 to play and plenty of time for 49er quarterback Joe Montana to come alive, Payton ran the ball 9 times for 52 yards in a 13-play, 66-yard touchdown drive that consumed 7:33. When he skirted left end for the final 17 yards and his second touchdown of the day, the 49ers had only 3:41 left.

"Unfortunately, when the 49ers beat us last year, they didn't show much courtesy or dignity," said Payton. "They said negative things about our offense after shutting us out. We thought about that all during the offseason. A team of All-Pros couldn't have stopped us."

Payton finished with 132 yards in 24 carries despite Ditka's game plan that called for passes on 15 of the first 20 plays.

"I was not going to come out and play them the way we played last year," said Ditka. "I was going to establish something and make them fear something and that was the pass. We were not going to run, run, run, punt."

The Bears averaged 5.9 yards on first down, more than doubling their 1984 output of 2.5 yards against the 49ers. They did it by passing on 13 of their 17 first downs in the first half and by running on 9 of their 13 first downs in the second half, a beautifully balanced performance.

The 49ers' only touchdown came on a 43-yard interception run by safety Carlton Williamson, who picked off an ill-advised McMahon pass.

The Bears' defense sacked Montana seven times, knocking the 49er receivers off their synchronized pass routes.

Defensive tackle Steve McMichael put three-time Pro Bowl guard Randy Cross into the dark ages with a ferocious rush that disrupted everything Montana tried to do. If Cross is in the Pro Bowl, McMichael was in another league against the 49ers.

End Richard Dent and linebacker Wilber Marshall had two sacks apiece. McMichael, strong safety Dave Duerson, and linebacker Otis Wilson had the others. Cornerbacks Mike Richardson and Leslie Frazier bumped the 49er receivers off their patterns.

"When we play our defense the way Buddy Ryan designs it, we can control teams," said Duerson.

McMahon needed only six plays to put the Bears up 7–0. He moved the offense without flanker Dennis McKinnon or tight end Emery Moorehead, stars of past games who were nursing leg injuries.

Instead, tight end Tim Wrightman found the open spaces in the

GAME 6

49er zones and caught passes for 24 and 26 yards in the first quarter when the Bears built a 13–0 lead.

By the time Butler's third field goal made it 16–0, the Bears had run 23 plays to only 7 for the 49ers. The shaky 49ers were penalized 13 times, including five times in six plays during their first possession of the third quarter.

On Williamson's interception, McMahon said he called the wrong pass route to split end Willie Gault. The play was supposed to be a pass to fullback Matt Suhey. McMahon was blitzed by linebacker Todd Shell and safety Ronnie Lott covered Suhey. McMahon thought Lott had left an open middle. But Gault wasn't there and William-

son was. It was the only thing that made the game close.

"You have to use the world champions as a barometer," said Ditka. "We took a giant step when we beat the Raiders last year when they were world champions. Hopefully, we'll take a giant step by beating the 49ers."

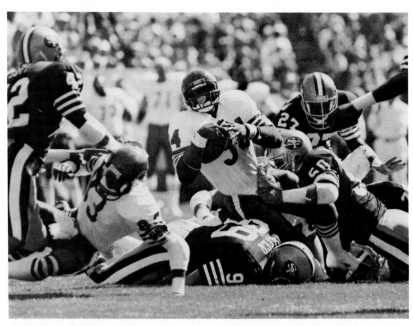

Walter Payton lunges for an extra yard against San Francisco. Payton scored twice and gained 132 yards as the Bears avenged their 1985 NFC championship game loss to the 49ers. (Tribune photo by Charles Cherney)

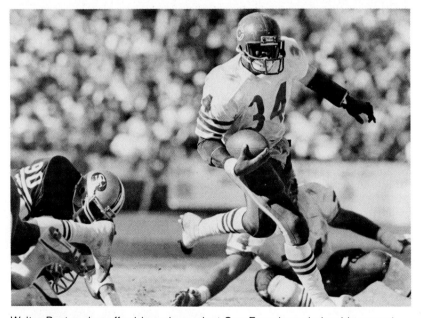

Walter Payton rips off a big gain against San Francisco during his record nine-game streak of 100-yard games. The Bears controlled the ball with Payton's running to wrap up a 26–10 victory over the 49ers. (Tribune photo by Charles Cherney)

Perry clears way for 7–0 Bears

By Don Pierson

The Bears thrilled the nation with their P-formation Oct. 21.

William Perry turned the Green Bay Packer goal line into a launching pad for new football concepts, scoring the winning touchdown in a 23–7 victory that kept the Bears undefeated.

The 325-pound defensive tackle, who said he weighs 308, lined up as a fullback on the wing three times at the goal line.

Twice, he blocked a gigantic path for Walter Payton to score. He broke a 7–7 tie with a 1-yard plunge himself in the second quarter.

"I said I wanted to help the team any way I could," said the No. 1 draft choice, who nearly flattened the football with a joyous spike after his touchdown.

Perry's next assignment might have to be quarterback, a development which isn't as funny.

The Bears' Jim McMahon had to leave the game with 10 minutes left because of a sprained right foot. But coach Mike Ditka was more worried about a sore rear end that has bothered McMahon all week.

"You should see the bruise. Yes, I'm concerned," said Ditka.

Except for a safety on a sack by linebacker Otis Wilson, all the scoring was done in the first half, allowing a national television audience to fall asleep in peace after Perry's performance.

"I felt like I was stealing on that second TD. I walked into the end zone," said Payton.

"Gain 100 pounds or forget about it," said regular fullback Matt Suhey.

On both of Payton's touchdowns, Perry knocked Packer linebacker George Cumby into football trivia.

"I only have one obligation and that's to block the linebacker," said Perry. "Whoever else got in the way I took him out, too. Cumby didn't say anything. I think I rung his bell."

Not since George Halas unveiled the T-formation has anything caused such commotion. It was the only thing that seemed to rouse the Soldier Field crowd of 65,095, which was quiet throughout another convincing victory by the 7–0 Bears.

Perhaps the Bears' four fumbles in the first half kept the fans from enjoying themselves, although four interceptions off Packer quarterbacks Lynn Dickey and Randy Wright evened the turnover ratio and set up the win.

The Bears thoroughly beat up the Packers, knocking out both Dickey and Wright while controlling both lines of scrimmage. Payton gained 112 yards in 25 carries. The fights and near-fights between plays were a great commercial for the Nov. 3 rematch in Green Bay.

"Mike and Forrest [Gregg] don't have the greatest desire to like each other and it stems to the players," said defensive tackle Steve McMichael.

The Bears got off to a bad start when they were called for a fumble on their first snap. Center Jay Hilgenberg and McMahon argued vehemently that Hilgenberg had not snapped the ball before the Packers jumped offsides. But the fumble stood.

"I hear the TV caught me saying some bad things," said Hilgenberg. "I hope my parents were in the kitchen at the time."

Safety Gary Fencik got the ball back on an interception at the goal line when Dickey hurried a pass to tight end Paul Coffman. Dickey was under pressure from Wilson.

A fumble by Suhey set up the night's first score, a 27-yard pass from Dickey to James Lofton, who beat cornerback Mike Richardson.

The Bears blew a chance to tie it when receiver Dennis McKinnon was stripped by cornerback Mark Lee at the 11-yard line. But Richardson got the ball back with the Bears' second interception and Payton's 2-yard plunge behind Perry tied it at 7.

The Bears got close again on a rare reverse on a punt, another trick up the long sleeve of Ditka.

"I haven't seen a reverse on a punt for 10 years," said Ditka.

Dennis Gentry took a handoff from Ken Taylor and ran 48 yards to the 10. Moments later, however, Payton fumbled when stripped by Lee.

On the next play, the shaky Dickey threw an interception straight at linebacker Wilber Marshall, who covered Coffman like a blanket.

Three plays later, Perry scored his touchdown, landing on tackle Keith Van Horne.

"I was saying, 'Pass it. Pass it,'" said Van Horne.

The Bears drove 86 yards for their final touchdown and took the rest of the night for granted.

"Speaking for myself, I got lethargic," said guard Tom Thayer. "I played more not to lose than to win. I was disappointed in myself."

Dickey, who had begged Gregg to take him out of the lineup earlier this season, left with a bruised thigh in the second quarter. Wright was replaced by Jim Zorn in the fourth quarter when Wilson's safety kept the Bears in the league scoring lead by one point.

The Bears also used three quarterbacks as Ditka went to Steve Fuller and then rookie

GAME 7

Mike Tomczak for a play that backfired on the snap.

The Bear interceptions completely erased any ideas the Packers had of being respectable. The Packer running game also was shut down to a 3.7-yard average.

"The defense was tremendous and a key to the football game," said Ditka.

Ditka passed up a short field goal by going for it on fourth down at the 4-yard line with the score 21–7. Perry was in on third down and Cumby got under his block. Ditka said a field goal never crossed his mind.

Ditka also left Payton in the game until the end, saying he didn't remember whether he asked him to take a rest.

"Mentally, we were unsharp on offense," said Ditka.

He said Perry could remain a fixture in short yardage.

"It's a good possibility until they put somebody in there bigger than he is to fill up the hole," said Ditka.

"You can't forget about Matt Suhey," pleaded Payton. "He would do just as good. Maybe the hole wouldn't be so wide, that's all."

Thayer said he heard a Packer linebacker daring Perry to run.

"He said, 'Come at me, big boy,'" said Thayer.

That's exactly what the Bears are doing to everyone in the National Football League, and having fun on the way.

William "the Refrigerator" Perry starts downfield on kickoff coverage against Green Bay Oct. 21. With the "Monday Night Football" audience watching, Perry scored his first pro TD on a 1-yard run in the Bears' 23–7 victory. (Tribune photo by Ed Wagner Jr.)

Oh, are we 8–0?

By Don Pierson

The Bears won the first half of the National Football League season Oct. 27 and decided to look at it as half empty rather than half full.

They did admit they aren't half bad after their 27–9 victory over the Vikings in Soldier Field. But on a day when the Los Angeles Rams' loss to the San Francisco 49ers made the Bears the only 8–0 team, they preferred to dwell on their imperfections.

They complained of poor execution on a day when they half killed the team that used to dominate the NFC Central Division the way they are doing.

They refused to claim they have the title wrapped up on a day when the 0–8 Tampa Bay Buccaneers were mathematically eliminated.

"Not when Detroit beats Miami and goes to 5–3. We have to play them twice," said coach Mike Ditka. "Plus, Green Bay next week will come after us."

"We should have scored 40 points," said tackle Keith Van Horne.

"What today showed is we have a lot of ways to win. If we put it all on the right track, we can be pretty darn good," said Ditka.

Quarterback Jim McMahon needed only seven plays to put the Vikings down 7–0 on a 32-yard touchdown pass to flanker Dennis McKinnon on an audible. Then the defense treated the Vikings like a cigarette butt under their heels.

Kevin Butler kicked field goals before and after the Vikings scored their only touchdown with help from a 27-yard pass interference penalty against Shaun Gayle.

In the third quarter, lineback-

Dennis Gentry bolts for a touchdown against the Vikings Oct. 27. (Tribune photo by Bob Langer)

er Otis Wilson returned an interception caused by end Richard Dent 23 yards for a touchdown to make it 20–7.

Linebacker Wilber Marshall ended a Viking threat with an interception at the 3-yard line later in the third period.

When Walter Payton caught a 20-yard screen pass from McMahon for a touchdown with 9:36 to play, the Vikings pulled starting quarterback Tommy Kramer and packed their bags.

"I think they let us score from way out because they didn't want William Perry to get in the backfield," said Payton.

Perry played no offense, but the Refrigerator did get into the Viking backfield to stop Kramer cold. He got the first sack of his

career and the first of the game against Kramer.

"It was better than scoring a TD," said Perry. "It was much better."

Before it was over, the Bears had five interceptions, matching their 1984 total of 21. Otis Wilson sacked Kramer twice and Mike Hartenstine sacked Wade Wilson once. Dent was penalized for unsportsmanlike conduct and then complained that Kramer was shoving him.

"The Bears are certainly deserving winners," said Minnesota coach Bud Grant, who should know one when he sees one. But Grant stopped short in his praise of the Bears, a team that seems more interested in winning games than friends.

Grant has played the Rams and the 49ers, but wouldn't comment on how the Bears stack up. "That's for you people to decide," he said.

Kramer was limited to 176 yards passing and Wade Wilson to 60. The Vikings ran only 14 times for 30 yards.

Kramer had 436 yards against the Bears Sept. 19, much of it after squirting through the rush and stepping up in the pocket. Perry discouraged that move this time after Ditka encouraged defensive coordinator Buddy Ryan to let his 308-pound No. 1 draft choice play.

Perry did not start on defense but played most of the game.

"I mentioned it to somebody and they responded," said Ditka of his suggestion to Ryan.

Ryan has been reluctant to use Perry, just as he was reluctant to use star linebackers Wilson and Marshall when they were rookies.

Ryan put Perry over center Dennis Swilley in the Bears' special "46" formation. Usually, tackle Dan Hampton plays over

the center. This time, Hampton moved over guard in place of Hartenstine. Steve McMichael also played over a guard and Dent rushed from outside.

"Ming [McMichael] and I have a quicker outside rush," said Hampton. "William is the guy who will take the center and move him back three or four yards. He's like a wave coming at you."

"We didn't have a chance to use the reverse to him," said Ditka. "We'll get to it next week."

When will Perry pass?

"As soon as he jumps over the goal post," said Ditka.

The Vikings' defense tossed their own version of the "46" at the Bears with less success.

"That defense is only as good as the personnel," said fullback Matt Suhey.

Payton ran for 118 yards in only 19 carries.

"We didn't block a soul and he gets 118 yards," said Van Horne.

The running again enabled the Bears to control the clock as they do better than anyone else. They had the ball for 34:42. "We wanted to keep it away from Kramer," said Van Horne.

For that, Kramer should have been thankful.

Safety Dave Duerson intercepted him first, and then Wilson broke open the game after Dent grabbed Kramer's arm as he threw.

"Somebody tipped it, and I just tried to get outside. I beat that guy to the corner [tackle Tim Irwin]. It would be embarrassing if a fat offensive lineman caught me," said Wilson.

Marshall's interception at the goal line kept Kramer from closing in on the 20–7 lead. He took the ball away from Darrin Nelson. Marshall later intercepted Wade Wilson for his fourth theft of the season, twice 1984's total

by the free agent he replaced, Al Harris.

"I guess he showed he does know a little bit about football," said Ditka.

"I'm starting to feel like I know what they're doing back there," said Marshall.

Free agent rookie Ken Taylor got an interception against Wade Wilson after replacing injured Mike Richardson in the first quarter. Richardson strained a hamstring muscle.

The Bears were less critical of their pass blocking. McMahon got out of the game without a sack. Steve Fuller took over with 8:33 left and was sacked for a safety by Neil Elshire. McMahon and Fuller were nursing sore backs.

"We talked about having two hurt quarterbacks, and we couldn't afford to have them touched," said Ditka. "They responded to the challenge."

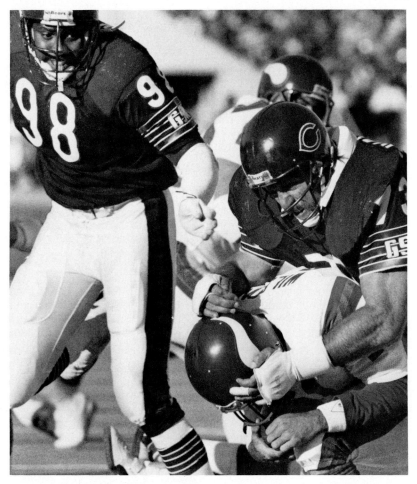

Take no prisoners, advises defensive end Tyrone Keys (98) as teammate Mike Hartenstine applies the sack to Minnesota quarterback Wade Wilson. (Tribune photo by Bob Langer)

Payton rescues a sorry show

By Don Pierson

Walter Payton could have been a great fighter, too. Fortunately for the Bears, he reminded everyone Nov. 3 that it still takes great players to win football games.

Payton's 27-yard touchdown run with 10:31 to play beat the Green Bay Packers 16–10 and kept the Bears undefeated.

It was their closest call of the season, and they had to call on Payton to pull it out. He obliged with 192 yards on 28 carries in a performance that awed his teammates and kept 55,343 fans in Lambeau Field from thinking they were watching pro wrestling.

"I thought Payton's exhibition was maybe as good as I've ever seen a guy with a football under his arm play," said coach Mike Ditka.

Not even William "the Refrigerator" Perry could upstage Payton on a day when Perry caught a touchdown pass from quarterback Jim McMahon to put the Bears ahead 7–3 in the first half.

It was Payton who told Perry where to line up before the defensive tackle put his 308 pounds into slow motion toward the flat.

"I got too close to the line, and Walter told me to step back a half step," said Perry. "I had to keep a straight face when I got on the line."

Perry's touchdown forced many of the most ardent Packer backers to crack smiles. Perry had burst onto the national scene Oct. 21 against the Packers on Monday night television by blasting Green Bay linebacker George Cumby into the end zone in a 23–7 Bears' victory.

This time, Cumby again was victimized by Perry, who became the P-formation-with-man-in-motion—yet another spinoff from the T-formation playbook popularized by the late George Halas.

"We ran against that same play in practice," said disappointed Packers' coach Forrest Gregg.

"They saw him coming and got out of the way," said Ditka.

They saw Payton coming, too, and could do nothing about it. The 192 yards was his 13th 100-yard performance in 20 games against the Packers.

He was the perfume in a game that was nasty before it started. When the Bears arrived at Lambeau Field, a bag of fertilizer awaited them in the locker room with a signed note from a Wisconsin radio station: "Here's what you guys are full of."

If it didn't serve to rile up the Bears' players, defensive tackle Dan Hampton said, "It ticked off Ditka."

"They played about as hard as I was excited," said Ditka.

On the ninth play of the game, Packers' cornerback Mark Lee was ejected after he ran Payton out of bounds and completely over the Bears' bench eight yards away.

On the second play, Payton fumbled, and when the Packers recovered in a pile-up, new Green Bay safety Ken Stills leveled McMahon with a block.

There were six personal fouls in the first half, four by the Packers. One was a particularly cheap late hit by Stills on Bears' fullback Matt Suhey that Gregg endorsed.

"I don't mind that. He took a crack at somebody. That's aggressive football," said Gregg.

The Bears congratulated themselves for keeping relatively cool.

"Tempers flare," said Ditka. "They had some new kids. You don't like to see it, especially when they cheap-shot a guy like Payton, who has given as much to the game as anyone. I'm sure the kid didn't mean it."

"By the end, there was something going on every play," said safety Dave Duerson. "Let's face it, it wasn't clean on either side."

It remained for Payton to lift it out of the gutter. He even wrapped it up with nice words by absolving the Packers of intent to maim.

"I don't think so. Forrest Gregg was a class player," said Payton.

The Packers sacked McMahon four times and held the Bears to 58 yards passing despite using three new players in their secondary. McMahon's pass to Perry was one of the better throws of his 9-for-20 day.

Ditka called it "by far our toughest game. They played us right to the teeth."

For Payton, it was one of his finest days at the office.

"I knocked the crap out of Payton. He's such a good athlete that he just kept on going," said Packers' linebacker Brian Noble.

The Packers had taken a 10–7 lead on a 55-yard pass from quarterback Jim Zorn to running back Jessie Clark against a blitz late in the third quarter.

The Bears had closed to 10–9 when defensive tackle Steve McMichael sacked Zorn for a safety, the most common way for defensive tackles to score before Perry.

The safety was set up when Packer receiver Phillip Epps unwisely made a fair catch of a high 45-yard punt by the Bears' Maury Buford at the Green Bay 4-yard line instead of giving it a chance to bounce into the end zone.

When Packer punter Joe Pro-

GAME9

kop followed the safety with a short free kick and McKinnon returned it 16 yards to the Green Bay 49, the Packers were set up for the kill.

Payton went left for 7 yards. Then McMahon saw linebacker Mike Douglass blitzing and audibled to a pass over the middle to tight end Tim Wrightman, who took it 17 yards to the 27.

Ditka called for a toss to Payton to the left, but the Packers were stacked and McMahon audibled to a "power lead play" behind tackle Keith Van Horne on the right.

Payton cut it up, bounced off Noble at the 20-yard line and outran the Packers' secondary to the end zone.

With 7:38 left, Gregg warmed up quarterback Lynn Dickey on the sideline, but he never put him in. Zorn finished the game by consistently underthrowing open receivers. James Lofton caught only one pass for 9 yards, even though the Bears were playing rookie Ken Taylor at one cornerback.

"We were surprised Dickey didn't come in," said safety Gary Fencik. "Obviously, they needed something."

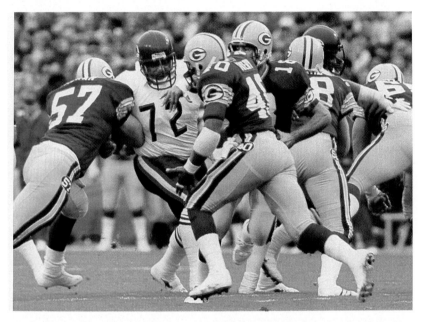

Wiliam Perry (72) tries to shake off a block and get at Green Bay's Eddie Lee Ivery before the Packer running back receives the handoff from quarterback Lynn Dickey (18). (Tribune photo by Jerry Tomaselli)

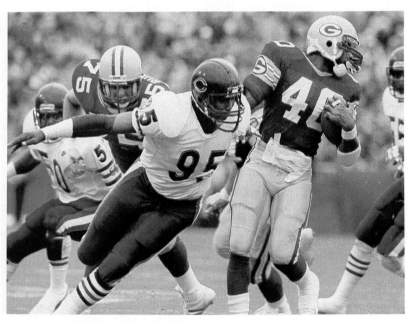

Defensive end Richard Dent led the league in sacks in 1985 with 17. Here he zeroes in on Green Bay's Eddie Lee Ivery (40). (Tribune photo by Bob Langer)

Bears' basics blow Lions away

By Don Pierson

As soon as the Detroit Lions won the toss and chose the wind Nov. 10 in Soldier Field, the Bears used them for a runway.

They took off like a jumbo jet into the 21-mile-an-hour gale from the north and blew the Lions away 24–3.

Quarterback Steve Fuller ran for two touchdowns against the wind, and Walter Payton and Matt Suhey ran like the wind.

The unbeaten Bears already had captured the Windy City. Now, they have harnessed it. They are flying so high at 10–0 that they can clinch the National Football Conference Central Division title by beating the Cowboys Nov. 17 at Irving, Texas.

The Bears barely had to get off the ground to beat the Lions. Payton and Suhey combined for 209 yards rushing, and William Perry rushed only the Lions' unlucky quarterback, Eric Hipple.

Twice, Hipple ducked smaller Bears only to have the 308-pound Perry flatten him for two of the four sacks registered by the vicious Bear defense.

Wind cannot stop the Bears, nor can rain, nor cold, nor lack of first-string quarterback or receivers.

They are a team built on a solid foundation of linemen who block and tackle against the wind as well as with it. The way they manhandled the Lions on the line of scrimmage revealed their true strength perhaps better than any of their previous victories.

Center Jay Hilgenberg, guards Mark Bortz and Tom Thayer, tackles Jimbo Covert and Keith Van Horne and tight end Tim Wrightman made holes wide enough for Perry, not to mention Payton and Suhey.

Defensive linemen Dan Hampton, Steve McMichael, Richard Dent and Perry and linebackers Mike Singletary, Otis Wilson and Wilber Marshall closed holes up front that enabled the defense to allow a season-low 106 yards.

"I wanted them to get only about 75," said a disappointed Singletary.

Just when Jim McMahon seemed to be the only valuable player, Fuller proved that sometimes all a Bear quarterback has to do is hand off.

To prove how well things are going for the Bears, Fuller admitted he didn't even carry the slippery ball into the end zone on the opening touchdown from the one-foot line. The Lions protested, but the missed fumble wasn't the turning point.

Suhey with 102 yards and Payton with 107 yards each reached 100 for the first time since Suhey had 113 and Payton 106 against Tampa Bay Nov. 20, 1983.

Just when flanker Dennis McKinnon and tight end Emery Moorehead needed a breather along with McMahon to nurse aches and pains, any plans to pass were swept out the window anyway.

"When we woke up this morning and saw the waves on Lake Michigan going up, we knew it would be a hard day to pass the ball," said Payton.

The Lions simply had no chance and didn't have the ball for even a third of the time. The Bears used up an astonishing 41:02 of the 60 minutes on offense, including 21:14 against the wind in the first and third quarters, when the Lions knew they would be running right at them.

The Lions did nothing to ruin their reputation as the worst team in the league against the run.

"They have been a zone team, bending and not breaking. Seeing that wind and wet and a new quarterback, I expected them to maybe come after me a little more," said Fuller.

"With that wind, you can't fool them because you can't loosen them up with deep passes," said Payton.

Instead, the Lions got fooled by the Bears' "influence plays" up the middle, where Hilgenberg did a job on Detroit nose tackle Doug English.

"Mike [Ditka] told me to just go the wrong way and don't block anybody, just what I normally do," said the modest Hilgenberg.

"Once Coach Ditka sees the film, Jay is going to get a game ball," said Thayer.

The Bears opened with 21 consecutive runs, using a minimum of different plays.

"That was pretty much what we said would happen. It doesn't always work the way you design it," said Ditka.

Fuller completed 7 of only 13 passes for 113 yards. He was 2 for 2 against the wind, including a 23-yarder to Wrightman that Ditka called "incredible." It kept the final touchdown drive alive.

Hipple completed only 8 of 17 passes and tried only 7 against the wind. Two were intercepted.

The Lions averted the shutout in the third quarter after Fuller tried an ill-advised lateral to receiver Willie Gault that was fumbled and led to a 34-yard field goal.

The Lions' longest drive was 24 yards, and it ended on downs at the Bear 23 in the third quarter. The Bears were ahead 14–0, enough to make the Lions feel desperate and make most of the

53,467 chilled fans feel confident enough to leave.

When the Lions took the wind and kicked off to the Bears, they expected to get the ball eventually. But the Bears ran 17 plays to only 7 for the Lions in the first quarter.

When the Bears got to the 4-yard line on a drive that consumed 8:22, they needed seven plays to score, including a hold-ing penalty on Detroit's Roosevelt Barnes. Perry lined up on three of the seven plays, but was used only as a decoy in motion when Fuller scored his phantom touchdown.

With the wind in the second quarter, Calvin Thomas made it 14–0 on a 7-yard draw play. The Bears caught the Lions in a blitz, and Payton made an impromptu block on free safety William Graham that sprung it.

"Almost killed the guy," said Ditka. "It's not his job to block the free safety in the hole, but he made the play."

Runs of 17 yards by Suhey and 10 by Payton set up the Bears' final touchdown in the third quarter. It was scored on a 5-yard bootleg by Fuller after a fake to Payton that left the Lions tackling nothing but air.

Richard Dent, Steve McMichael (76) and jubilant Otis Wilson (55) surround Lions' quarterback Eric Hipple (17) after sacking him in the Bears' 37–17 victory at Detroit. (Tribune photo by Bob Langer)

Bears annihilate Cowboys

By Don Pierson

The Bears wrung the necks of the Dallas Cowboys Nov. 17 and tightened the chokehold they have on the National Football League. They are beginning to put the squeeze on history.

They smashed the Cowboys 44–0 in a game that was just as close as the score indicated. They played the defense of their dreams and handed the Cowboys their worst defeat ever.

The Bears clinched the National Football Conference's Central Division title earlier than anyone ever has clinched a title in a 16-game schedule. Then they started talking about home-field advantage for the playoffs, as if they needed one. It was their 11th straight victory, matching their 11–0 season in 1942.

They proved they can thrive without injured quarterback Jim McMahon, who, after all, does not play defense.

Bears' coach Mike Ditka beat his mentor, Dallas coach Tom Landry, and called it "no big deal." But he gave game balls to every Bear on the team and promised to gold-plate one for back-up quarterback Steve Fuller. The Bears had not defeated Dallas in six tries since 1971, when Ditka played for Landry.

"Everybody wanted it, more so for Mike," said running back Walter Payton, who made history of his own with 132 yards to reach his ninth 1,000-yard season. He had been tied at eight with former Steelers' star Franco Harris.

"It seemed like the energy and electricity from him just flowed into the other players," Payton added. "This one was for Mike."

"He downplayed it, but it was written on his face," said safety

Willie Gault caught only one TD pass during the 1985 regular season, but he had 33 receptions and averaged more than 21 yards a catch. (Tribune photo by Charles Cherney)

Dave Duerson.

"I would like to see him smile," said Fuller. "Late in the game I said, 'I think it's okay for you to go ahead and let out a big smile.' And he still wouldn't."

The way the Bears played defense was no laughing matter. Defensive end Richard Dent and cornerback Mike Richardson scored the Bears' first two touchdowns on interceptions, the first off starter Danny White and the second off sub Gary Hogeboom.

Linebacker Otis Wilson knocked White cold in the first half. When White came back, Wilson put him out again with a "jammed neck."

"I put the wood on him," said Wilson.

Richardson intercepted Hogeboom's second pass for his touchdown, and cornerback Leslie Frazier intercepted Hogeboom's third pass to set up a touchdown sneak by Fuller before the half that made it 24–0.

Kevin Butler hit a 44-yard field goal in the first half and kept the pressure on with field goals of 46 and 22 yards in the third and fourth quarters. The long one came after William Perry was penalized for trying to pick up Payton and shot-put him into the end zone from the 2-yard line.

It is illegal to aid a runner like that, although Payton might have been the first player to score a touchdown while carrying a refrigerator on his back.

"I didn't know what was going on," said Payton.

Neither did Perry, who said, "If they didn't call me for holding or something, I believe we both would have got into the end zone."

Ditka called off the dogs in the final 10 minutes, letting rookie quarterback Mike Tomczak direct scoring drives that ended in a 17-yard touchdown run by sub Calvin Thomas and a 16-yarder by another sub, Dennis Gentry.

The Cowboys had suffered only one other regular-season shutout, 38–0 against St. Louis in 1970, again when Ditka played for Landry.

"Our defense, what can you say?" asked Ditka. "They took the football game away from them. It was just a matter of the offense mopping up. It was awe-

GAME11

some to see."

For Landry, it was so awful to see that he failed to recognize what he had seen.

"I would like to see what would have happened if we had played a good football game. You can't take anything away from the Bears, but we didn't play good football," said Landry.

Like his team, he missed the point. The Cowboys had trouble playing good football because the Bears were stuffing it down their throats.

The Cowboys never made more than two first downs in a series. They gained only 171 yards. Tony Dorsett got only 44, including 22 on the first play. Tony Hill, the league's leading receiver entering the game, caught two passes for 15 yards. Tight end Doug Cosbie left the contest in the first half with a twisted neck.

After Maury Buford's fourth straight great punt had pinned the Cowboys on their 2-yard line late in the first quarter, defensive end Dan Hampton cartwheeled tackle Jim Cooper with a swing of his right arm, leaped into White's face in the end zone and batted a pass into the air.

"I thought Hampton had knee problems, but I see he don't if he can jump that high," said Dent, who leaped higher and grabbed the ball like a rebound. "I didn't think anybody else noticed where the ball was. My intention was getting it before anybody else noticed it."

Dent made a 1-yard lunge for the touchdown that was the beginning of the end.

Dent sacked White on the Cowboys' next play, and Wilson sacked him again on the play after that. On the second play of the next series, Wilson drilled White to the floor of Texas Stadium and Hogeboom came in.

On his second series, the Bears shifted from a 4-3 defensive front to a 3-4 just before the snap. Such shifting fouled up the Cowboys' blocking assignments all day. Wilson and Dent blitzed and Hogeboom threw right to Richardson.

"Mike was standing there where the guy maybe should have been. Pumped it right to him," said Singletary. "Same play we'd been dreaming about."

"Yes, when things like that start happening, you begin to wonder," said Richardson, whose return covered 36 yards.

"It's going to take quite an effort by somebody to get in our way right now," said center Jay Hilgenberg.

"We're destined," said Duerson.

"This team hasn't reached its potential yet," said Payton. "I keep saying that."

And the Bears keep proving it.

Mike Richardson gets ready to receive a Bear hug from Otis Wilson after Richardson's 36-yard touchdown run with an interception in the 44–0 rout of Dallas on Nov. 17. (Tribune photo by Ed Wagner Jr.)

William Perry (72) tries to give the Bears—and Walter Payton—a big lift against the Cowboys. Perry was penalized, but the Bears won 44–0. (Tribune photo by Ed Wagner Jr.)

Dan Hampton penetrates the Dallas offensive line and knocks down a Danny White pass in the end zone during the Bears' 44–0 rout of the Cowboys Nov. 17. (Tribune photo by Bob Langer)

Linebacker Wilber Marshall (58) tips a pass by Dallas quarterback Danny White during the Bears' 44–0 victory. (Tribune photo by Ed Wagner Jr.)

Bears zero in on perfection

By Don Pierson

The Bears are painting the 1985 season by the numbers. The picture looks so good the artists seem to be cheating. Are these victories any harder than they look?

They won their 12th in a row Nov. 24 in Soldier Field when they brushed aside the Atlanta Falcons 36–0. Soon, the zeroes might become understood. The Bears beat the Dallas Cowboys 44. They beat the Falcons 36.

This time, it was Walter Payton tightroping on a magnificent 40-yard touchdown run that got the numbers moving. While lesser artists surely would have slipped outside the line, Payton somehow managed to stay in-bounds.

William Perry, Calvin Thomas and Thomas Sanders also plunged for shorter touchdowns. Kevin Butler kicked two field goals and defensive lineman Henry Waechter scored a safety.

The numbers get more impressive every week. Only two other National Football League teams have won 12 games at the start of their seasons. The 1934 Bears were 13–0. The 1972 Miami Dolphins were 17–0 following their Super Bowl triumph.

Beating the Falcons guaranteed the Bears of being the home team for the first National Football Conference playoff game. One more victory ensures the Bears that Soldier Field would be the site of the NFC title game, should they win the first playoff game.

"I didn't know if this would be hard or easy," said coach Mike Ditka. "The way our defense is playing, it seems nothing is too hard."

The Bear defenders allowed the Falcons past the 50-yard line once, so they insisted there is room for improvement. They gave up minus-22 yards passing and added two interceptions and five sacks, but the Falcons did complete three whole passes, two by starter and finisher David Archer and one by middle reliever Bob Holly.

"Archer didn't really impress me as far as a quarterback who could beat you," said linebacker Otis Wilson.

A field goal by Detroit Nov. 10 in a 24–3 victory is the only score against the Bears in the last 13 quarters. They have held 9 of 12 opponents to one touchdown.

The last time the Bears shut out two teams in a row was in 1942.

"Yeah, but they lost the championship in 1942," said Ditka. "I don't want to hear that crap."

Payton gained 102 yards in three quarters before Ditka called up the reserves, who immediately poured it on for the second week in a row.

It was Payton's seventh 100-yard game in a row, tying the NFL record held by O. J. Simpson and Earl Campbell.

"As callous a guy as I am, I'm determined to get him his eighth next week and his ninth, because when his name goes down, it will go down alone above those other backs," said Ditka.

Payton's touchdown followed two field goals by Butler. He strung out the defense and cut upfield behind a block by Thomas, who was playing for injured fullback Matt Suhey.

"Incredible. The guy's hurting. Didn't practice all week. He didn't even warm up, hardly," said Ditka.

"I thought he was just going to make the first down and slide out of bounds," said Fuller.

After Fuller unloaded 20- and 50-yard passes to split end Willie Gault on consecutive plays to the 1-yard line, "the Refrigerator" leaped into the south end zone to make it 20–0 in the first half.

He made a sign at Soldier Field prophetic: "Sir William Perry, Discoverer of South Goal."

Perry took off from the 2-yard line as defensive lineman Dan Benish grabbed his ankles.

It was the third touchdown of the season for the 302-pound Perry, the first by going over the pile. He bulled through against the Packers, tiptoed in on a pass reception against the Packers and now, up in the sky.

The second half was unnecessary if not unfair. On the first play, Archer saw defensive end Richard Dent in his face and tossed a pass to cornerback Leslie Frazier, who returned the interception to the Atlanta 21.

When the Bear offense couldn't make it past the 4-yard line, Atlanta coach Dan Henning sent in Holly at quarterback. On third down, Dent stripped Holly of the ball in the end zone and Mike Hartenstine recovered for the Bears at the 2-yard line.

Fullback Thomas scored untouched to run it to 27–0. Waechter added a safety against Holly as the Falcons insisted on trying to pass from their end zone and almost nowhere else.

Rookie running back Sanders scored his first pro touchdown to wrap it up and leave the Falcons to ponder whether they really are 8 points better than the Cowboys.

The Bears are left to ponder whether they can get any better in December and January than they were in November.

"I think the odds have started to go in our favor. The pressure goes on the other people playing us," said Ditka. "They are the

ones thinking, 'Stop 'em. Beat 'em.' That will be the pressure on the Dolphins next week."

"We can play better offensively, but I don't know how we can play any better on defense," said Ditka. "It's hard to believe those guys. They're like—what was it?—Sherman's army that marched through the South. They just ripped the stuffing out of everything in their way."

Payton said incentive remains

no problem because the picture is not yet complete. But he admitted there aren't many blank spaces left on the canvas.

"It's scary because you look at the points we're scoring and the way the defense is playing and the way the offense is rallying around whoever is in there and you wonder if you're that good or not and if you're playing anybody of good caliber," said Payton. "We watch people on

film and they look good. Then once we get on the field, I don't know if it's the intimidation factor of playing the Bears or people conceding getting beat or what.

"The latter part of the season will be real rough. But right now, this team has a tremendous amount of pride. For so long, Chicago has not had a winning team. Everybody here wants to keep the record unblemished."

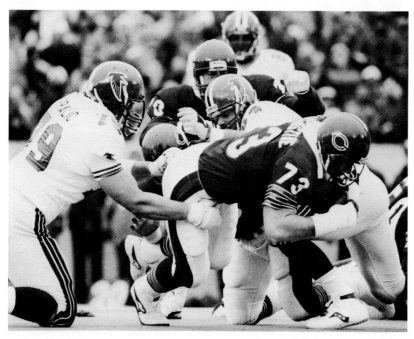

Mike Hartenstine dives for the goal line after recovering a fumble against Atlanta. He didn't make it into the end zone. (Tribune photo by Bob Langer)

Otis Wilson, Richard Dent and Reggie Phillips get a heroes' welcome from Soldier Field fans after the Bears' 36–0 defeat of the Atlanta Falcons on Nov. 24. (Tribune photo by Ed Wagner Jr.)

Bears squeezed in Miami vise

By Don Pierson

The Bears convinced the National Football League they are perfectly human Dec. 2 when the Miami Dolphins ruined their perfect season and preserved history for themselves with a 38–24 victory.

The Bears' 12-game winning streak and dreams of an undefeated season turned to a nightmare with a 31-point onslaught by quarterback Dan Marino and the Dolphins in the first half.

By the time the No. 1 defense in the league adjusted and Bears' coach Mike Ditka switched from Steve Fuller to Jim McMahon at quarterback, it was too late. The noisy Orange Bowl crowd of 75,594 counted down the seconds and hailed the 1972 Dolphins as the last unbeaten [17–0] team.

When the Bears gave up their fourth touchdown in the first half after a blocked punt at their own 6-yard line, Ditka screamed in frustration at defensive coordinator Buddy Ryan on the sidelines. But when it was over, Ditka was calm.

"Nobody's perfect and we proved it. Now it's what you do with it. Do you bounce back? We'll be back," said Ditka.

To a man, the Bears gave the Dolphins credit, but felt they beat themselves more than Marino did. Marino completed 14 of 27 passes for 270 yards and 3 touchdowns. He made big plays on five of six third downs in the first half, and the Dolphins scored the first five times they got the ball to take a 31–10 halftime lead.

The victory lifted the Dolphins into a first-place tie with the New England Patriots and the New York Jets in the American Football Conference's East Division.

Bear linebacker Mike Singletary sacks Dolphin quarterback Dan Marino Dec. 2 in Miami. The Dolphins handed the Bears their only regular-season loss, 38–24. (Tribune photo by Ed Wagner Jr.)

McMahon was sharp during warm-ups after a three-week layoff with a shoulder injury. But Ditka did not turn to him until Fuller limped off with a sprained left ankle with 12 minutes 47 seconds to play.

McMahon moved the Bears briefly until an interception by William Judson in the end zone with 6:12 left ended any hopes for a miracle.

Walter Payton got his record-breaking eighth 100-yard game in a row only because the Bears called time out three times in the final minute when the Dolphins had the ball. Payton finished with 121 yards in 23 carries and carried only 10 times in the first half.

"Walter Payton is the greatest football player to ever play the game. Other people who call themselves running backs can't carry his jersey," said Ditka.

Poor field position and turnovers set up four of the Dolphins' five touchdowns. In the first half, wide receiver Nat Moore caught two TD passes from Marino and running back Ron Davenport ran for two.

Of the defense, Ditka said: "I thought we could have adjusted earlier to some things. They beat our butts pretty good."

When receiver Mark Clayton caught a 42-yard touchdown pass that was tipped by Bears' defensive lineman Dan Hampton in the third quarter for their last points, the Dolphins knew it was their night.

It was the Bears' ninth straight loss on the road on "Monday Night Football." The 31 first-half points shattered a string of 13 scoreless quarters and were the most points scored against the Bears by halftime since the 1972 season opener. The 12 victories at the start of a regular season ranks as the third best in history behind the Dolphins' 14–0 in 1972 and the Bears 13–0 in 1934.

When the Bears pulled to 31–17 with 9:25 left in the third period, Ditka appeared to order an onside kick by Kevin Butler that rookie Alex Moyer recovered for the Dolphins at the Chicago 46.

Three plays later, Clayton caught his tipped pass.

"It was not an onside kick," Ditka said. "It was supposed to be a lob down to the 30-yard line, and Kevin didn't hit it well. But I take the blame."

The Dolphins scored three of their five touchdowns after getting the ball at the Chicago 25, Chicago 6 and Chicago 46.

Ditka chose to get into a shootut with Marino in the first half, and Marino won.

GAME 13

Payton did not carry the ball until the Bears were behind 10–7 with 5:56 left in the first quarter. When he did, he gained 14 yards in three carries. Then Ditka called a screen pass that Fuller overthrew, a play Ditka second-guessed. Dolphin linebacker Bob Brudzinski intercepted and Bear tackle Keith Van Horne was penalized for unnecessary roughness to set Marino up at the Chicago 25.

On third and 19, Marino hit Moore for 22 yards and soon it was 17–7.

The Bears closed to 17–10 after a Statue of Liberty handoff to Payton and throwback to Fuller backfired.

Then the Bears lost the game in the final 5 minutes of the half.

Marino faced a third down and 13 from his own 18. He rolled right against a 3-4 defense and found Mark Duper running open for a 52-yard gain.

Three plays later, it was third and 7. Again Marino rolled and found Clayton for 26 yards to the 1-yard line. Davenport scored to make it 24–10 with 1:57 left.

The Bears took over at their 20 and tried to move downfield by passing. Fuller was sacked and had to scramble on third down. When Maury Buford tried to punt, William Judson broke through the middle and blocked it.

It took Marino two plays to hit Moore and run it to 31–10.

"There's no question we helped them on their way," said center Jay Hilgenberg. "But the only thing that matters is the last game of the year."

"They were a better team than us," said tackle Jimbo Covert. "Tonight. It ain't the end of the world. On this day in history, they were better. Five or six weeks down the road, we might be better than them."

"I don't think it affects the achievements of the 1985 Bears," said safety Gary Fencik. "We have to take it as a positive. We're not infallible."

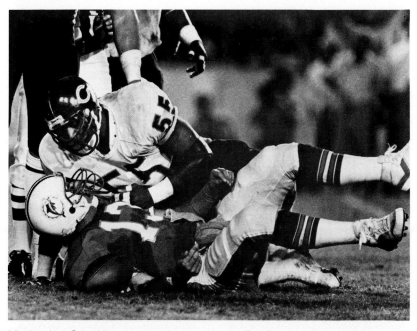

Linebacker Otis Wilson earned a spot in the Pro Bowl while terrorizing quarterbacks like Miami's Dan Marino. (Tribune photo by Ed Wagner Jr.)

Bears plod to another victory

By Don Pierson

Their homework is done, and the Bears still can't go out to play the way they would like. They are ready to graduate, and school isn't over yet.

They almost called in sick Dec. 8 before realizing the rules require a 16-game workload.

So as long as class was scheduled, the Bears showed up and passed another test. They beat the Indianapolis Colts 17–10 in their final appearance in Soldier Field before the start of the National Football Conference exams.

"I'm not unhappy," said coach Mike Ditka. "I kinda really thought it would be 7 or 10 or 13 points. I didn't think it would be a blowout like a lot of people. The main thing is we're going into the playoffs, and people are going to have to come here to play us."

The Bears have two more of these darned pop quizzes that don't count on the grade card. The fans just want to find out if the Bears know their assignments.

Walter Payton came through late in the third quarter to break a 3–3 halftime tie with a 16-yard touchdown run. He got 100 yards for the ninth time in a row just before the bell rang.

A 3-yard touchdown run by Calvin Thomas with 6:49 left provided a 17–3 cushion. It was enough to make the 61-yard roll-out touchdown pass from Colts' quarterback Mike Pagel to Wayne Capers three plays later no more than a conversation piece.

Both Chicago touchdowns followed great punts by Maury Buford that gave the Bears good field position.

The game was without turnovers on either side, proving perfection doesn't necessarily guarantee excitement. It was the first time all season the Bears had no takeaways or giveaways, so Buford's punting against the Colts' Rohn Stark was crucial.

Jim McMahon returned to start at quarterback for the Bears for the first time since Nov. 3. He completed 11 of 23 passes for 145 yards and no touchdowns. He even heard some boos from the crowd of 59,997 during the Bears' lowest-scoring first half since Oct. 6 at Tampa.

"He can't throw it and then run over and catch it," said Ditka.

"I didn't feel rusty. I felt I threw the ball well," said McMahon.

Perhaps McMahon's most significant play was a slide feet first at the end of a 14-yard scramble to the 12 to set up Kevin Butler's 20-yard field goal in the second quarter.

"My shoulder felt fine, and I even slid feet first. Surprised the heck out of me," said McMahon. "I got up and said, 'Did I do that?'"

Pagel played more like Miami's Dan Marino than the lowest-rated passer in the AFC in the first half. The Colts drove 72 yards with the opening kickoff. They didn't get any points out of it, but they didn't get down, either.

In the second half, the Bear defense held the Colts to only 14 plays while the Bear offense stretched its time of possession to 38:55.

Payton ran only six times in the first half and 20 in the second after, Ditka said, he "got nasty notes from the media saying, 'Run Payton.'"

On the first touchdown drive, McMahon called an audible on third and 1 from his 46 and threw a 7-yard quick out pass to Ken Margerum.

"Surprised everyone in the stadium," said center Jay Hilgenberg.

Payton's touchdown was on a trap play on third and 6 against five defensive backs.

Payton finished with 111 yards, 61 in the final quarter when the Bears ran 23 plays and the Colts ran only 6. Payton said he didn't feel the effects of a flu bout until after the game and cited "a block for Matt Suhey" as his most satisfying moment.

After Payton's touchdown, Buford boomed a 64-yard punt that was slowed by Shaun Gayle and downed by Dennis Gentry and Jim Morrissey on the 4-yard line.

With the crowd helping the defense and hindering Pagel's signal-calling, Stark was forced to punt out of his end zone. Even though he boomed a 55-yarder, the Bears' Keith Ortego returned it 15 yards to the Colts' 45.

Payton and Thomas ran on 10 of 11 plays, with Thomas scoring the clinching touchdown.

After Wilson nailed Pagel for the only sack of the day, Pagel faced third and 20. He eluded the blitzing Wilson and Mike Singletary and rolled to his right. When cornerback Mike Richardson bit on an out-pattern, Capers ran past him, and Pagel hit him for the touchdown.

There will be all kinds of discussion and speculation on momentum and incentive when the Bears travel to New York to play the Jets and to Detroit to play the Lions. None of it will mean anything until the playoffs. For the Bears, this is like detention for doing no more than clinching their division so early it wasn't fair.

76

Bears' pride too much for Jets

By Don Pierson

Magic returned to the Bears Dec. 14. They were able to take some windy Chicago weather on the road and turn Giants Stadium into a home-field disadvantage for the New York Jets.

Just for the heck of it, the Bears won 19–6 and made the Jets virtually disappear from the AFC East Division title picture.

Because it was advertised as meaningless, the Bears' victory was as impressive as any of their other 13 in an increasingly meaningful year.

"You don't need any motivation except pride," said defensive lineman Dan Hampton. "We don't care about wins and losses. We just want to play hard and play well."

Four field goals by Kevin Butler of 18, 31, 37 and 21 yards and one 7-yard touchdown pass from quarterback Jim McMahon to tight end Tim Wrightman was luxury for this defense.

With Jets quarterback Ken O'Brien trying to throw with a gusting 28-mile-an-hour wind at his back in the third quarter, end Richard Dent climbed on his back and forced two fumbles.

Earlier in that same decisive quarter, the Bears defied the wind to complete the longest play of the game, a 65-yard swing pass to Walter Payton. It set up Butler's second field goal, a 31-yarder that made the score 13–6.

The Jets held Payton to 53 yards on 28 carries. Eleven times, they stopped him for losses or no gain and ended his record string of 100-yard games at nine.

With Payton and the offense in check, Butler did it. His second field goal broke Mac Percival's 1968 club record of 25. His fourth, with only 17 seconds left to play, was attempted to rub out Bob Thomas' 1984 club record of 11 in a row, although the Jets might have thought Ditka was rubbing it in.

"We were just going for the record," Ditka said.

Butler's first two field goals were against the wind, which Butler claimed was increased by friendly Jets' attendants who raised a sliding gate in the east end of the stadium both times he got ready to kick.

"That gate would come up and you could feel that draft come in. Home-field advantage," Butler said. "We'd do it, too, if we had a gate."

Late in the third quarter, Butler turned down a chance for a 34-yard field goal after he saw the 31-yarder barely make it over the crossbar.

"I didn't think I could make it," Butler said. "I didn't want to hurt the team then. It was almost the fourth quarter and we got two more chances."

The Bears failed to gain on fourth down and gave the Jets the ball at the 18.

"They didn't have field position anyway," Ditka said.

It was the fifth time the Jets had taken possession in the third quarter. Their drives were for none, six, two, four and four yards in a magnificent display of defense.

The Jets scored on the first drive on a 55-yard field goal by Pat Leahy to close to 10–6 and get the capacity crowd of 74,752 excited. McMahon and Payton quieted things two plays later. Flanker Dennis McKinnon set a pick on linebacker Lance Mehl and left him scurrying after Payton down the sidelines.

The Jets chose the wind after they won the toss, but the Bears controlled the ball for 11 minutes 10 seconds, causing the strategy to backfire. When the Bears took the ball to start the third quarter, the Jets took the wind, hoping to make up the 10–3 deficit.

Wrightman had broken the 3–3 first-quarter tie on a 7-yard scoring pass, his first in the NFL. It followed two big breaks for the Bears on the first two plays of the second quarter.

First, officials said an apparent interception by Jets' safety Kirk Springs hit the ground. Then safety Lester Lyles was called for a personal foul when the Bears failed to gain on second and 10.

The Bears were not able to run as well against the wind in the third quarter as they were in the first because the Jets adjusted.

"They started overloading and blitzing us," McMahon said. "Tough to run against that."

"They were the best defense we've faced," said center Jay Hilgenberg. "We can do a lot better, though. They were just trying to stop No. 34 and have us beat them another way. Jim made some big plays."

A 23-yard pass to Willie Gault in the fourth quarter with the score 13–6 got the Bears out of a hole and enabled Cliff Thrift to down a punt by Maury Buford at the 4-yard line. It set up Butler's third field goal with 4:41 to play.

The Bears have held 11 of 15 opponents to 10 points or less, but after subpar performances the last two weeks, defensive coordinator Buddy Ryan required his players to take three classroom tests on the Jets' game. They passed the final exam in a breeze.

Ditka not swayed by win

By Don Pierson

History already says the 1985 Bears are one of the best football teams of all time. But the Bears are not yet interested in history.

Coach Mike Ditka said he is "terrified" their record-tying 15–1 regular season will soon be nothing more than history if they play as poorly in the playoffs as they did Dec. 22 in beating the Detroit Lions 37–17.

"We'll be the underdogs, no question about it," said Ditka. "Maybe we're doing too many 'Super Bowl Shuffles.'"

"We did that record five weeks ago," said receiver Willie Gault, who helped organize the "Super Bowl Shuffle." "Maybe there's too many McDonald's commercials, too many car commercials. It hasn't affected anybody's play. That's absurd."

"Heck, we won," said quarterback Jim McMahon. "I don't put any weight on that. It has nothing to do with our play."

Regardless of its accuracy, Ditka's tirade made certain the Bears will enter the playoffs with the same chip on their shoulders they had when they entered the season.

"If we would have killed them, maybe we would have been overconfident," said defensive lineman Dan Hampton.

From their receivers to their special-teams players, the Bears went away mad. Dennis Gentry returned the second-half kickoff 94 yards for the Bears' first touchdown, but Ditka groused about poor kickoff-return coverage and missed opportunities by the offense near the goal line.

It took a 50-yard pass by Walter Payton and a nice catch by Gault to finally get the offense into the end zone in the fourth quarter. In the playoffs, Ditka is afraid that might be too late.

"Say I'm concerned. Say I'm terrified. Anything you want," said Ditka.

For the second year in a row, the defense let the Lions spoil its quest to lead the league in pass defense. The Lions' 17 points kept the Bears from breaking the 16-game record of 195 points set by the Pittsburgh Steelers in 1978. The Bears allowed 198.

But if they didn't kill the Lions, the Bears nearly maimed them. As they have done consistently all season, they pounded the Lions physically, scoring 21 points in the final period when the forlorn Lions were thinking about Christmas.

"We couldn't beat a playoff team today," said Ditka. "We would have been eliminated."

Against the Lions, they didn't have to worry about playoff-caliber competition, even in the friendly Silverdome, with 74,042 fans alternately cheering and booing both teams. When William "the Refrigerator" Perry ran 59 yards with a fumble recovery to set up the Bears' final touchdown, it left everybody laughing.

Perry was caught at the Lions' 15 by tight end David Lewis, but not until the Fridge had secured a few more commercials.

The Bears' defense had provided a 30–10 cushion early in the final period when linebacker Ron Rivera became the 21st different Bear to score in '85.

Playing for the injured Mike Singletary, Rivera picked up a ball knocked loose by the remarkable Richard Dent and scored from the 5-yard line. Dent dislodged the ball from James Jones after a pass from quarterback Eric Hipple.

Singletary left the game in the third quarter with a sprained left knee that caused some anxious moments. But he said he was all right and could have returned to the game if necessary.

Ditka took McMahon [13 for 22, 194 yards] and Payton [17 rushes, 81 yards] out of the game early in the fourth period, but put them both back for the final touchdown after the Lions had moved to 30–17 with 11:01 left. Back-up quarterback Steve Fuller suffered a concussion, and rookie Mike Tomczak also played at quarterback before McMahon finished.

The Bears got into Detroit territory on seven of their first eight possessions. Maury Buford didn't have to punt until there were less than six minutes left in the game. But they couldn't score from scrimmage until the fourth quarter, when McMahon dived in after a 14-yard scramble.

The Bears built a 16–3 lead on three field goals by Kevin Butler (who added four PATs to set a Bears' season scoring record with 144 points) and Gentry's return, but Ditka and the players were upset over confusion and inefficiency near the goal line. Some of the anger was over execution, some over Ditka's play-calling.

"Took us until the fourth quarter to outscore our defense and special teams," said Ditka. "We talk about kickoff coverage, and we didn't cover. When the Lions needed to pass, they passed. Unless we blitzed, we couldn't get to the quarterback. We get near the end zone and settle for field goals.

"Where did we play well?"

Twice, McMahon threw interceptions near the goal line. On the first one, Detroit cornerback Bobby Atkins made a nice play. On the second, Gault did not adjust his route on a blitz, and

GAME16

McMahon threw right to cornerback Bruce McNorton.

"Willie broke the route. Jim threw where he was supposed to. He's not a mind-reader," said Ditka.

"I caught everything thrown to me," said Gault. "I made one mistake."

McMahon's touchdown scramble made it 23–10 and was followed two plays later by Dent's play against fullback Jones.

With Dent playing linebacker in the 3-4, Hipple passed in the flat to Jones, and Dent knocked the ball out of his hands. Rivera picked it up and scored.

Linebacker Wilber Marshall had knocked starting quarterback Joe Ferguson out of the game on the third play with a hit that should cure any thoughts about rolling out on the Bears. Marshall also forced the fumble that Perry picked up.

Dent collected two of the six sacks against Hipple, who replaced Ferguson and completed 22 of 44 passes for 287 yards.

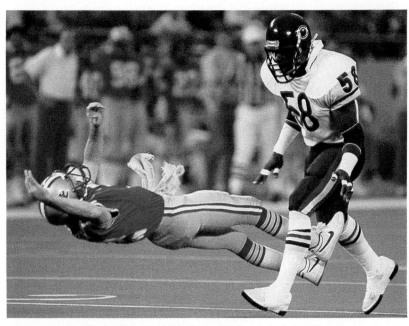

Wilber Marshall knocks out Lions' quarterback Joe Ferguson with a vicious tackle, which later cost him when NFL commissioner Pete Rozelle levied a $2,000 fine. (Tribune photo by Bob Langer)

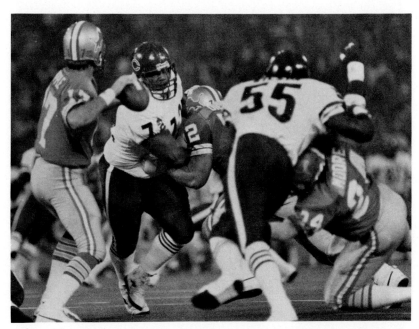

William Perry (72) and Otis Wilson (55) have Lions' quarterback Eric Hipple caught coming and going in the Bears' Dec. 22 victory at the Silverdome. (Tribune photo by Charles Cherney)

Linebacker Otis Wilson (55) and cornerback Mike Richardson put the crunch on an unlucky Lion Dec. 22. The visiting Bears romped 37–17 at the Pontiac Silverdome. (Tribune photo by Ed Wagner Jr.)

Jim McMahon takes the shortest route to the end zone against Detroit with this headlong dive. The Bears breezed to a 37–17 victory at Pontiac. (Tribune photo by Ed Wagner Jr.)

Bears knock Giants cold

By Don Pierson

The Bears haven't been fair all season, so why should they start now? The New York Giants were supposed to have a chance Jan. 5 in the National Football Conference semifinal game. They didn't. The Bears won 21–0 with a defense as cold-hearted as the weather that chilled 62,076 fans in Soldier Field.

William "the Refrigerator" Perry, all 304 pounds of him, even jumped on top of New York's 5-foot-7-inch running back, Joe Morris, and knocked him out of the game with a slight concussion. Morris returned, but at 5-6.

"I caught him with everything, everything I had," said Perry.

After Shaun Gayle's bizarre 5-yard punt return for a touchdown in the first quarter, the mean and nasty Bears rubbed it in.

Quarterback Jim McMahon's two touchdown passes to receiver Dennis McKinnon in the third quarter might provoke a letter from commissioner Pete Rozelle charging unnecessary conduct.

McMahon can point out he threw them against the wind while wearing gloves.

Defensive coordinator Buddy Ryan had promised a shutout.

"We believe every thought Buddy shares with us," said safety Dave Duerson.

Richard Dent, freed up by another new wrinkle in Ryan's scheme, sacked Giants' quarterback Phil Simms 3½ times. Simms was sacked six times, and the Giants punted after three plays nine of the first 11 times they had the ball.

Until the Giants gained 129 yards on their final two possessions, the Bears had held them to an average of 40 inches a play.

Morris gained 32 yards on only 12 carries. After a 14-yarder on his first attempt, he couldn't gain his height on each carry.

In a game of defense, Dent left no doubt about who was the most spectacular player on the field. He also led the Bears in tackles with 6½, running down Morris from behind and preventing cutbacks.

The Giants came into the game with the No. 2 defense in the NFL and left knowing that Avis is a lot closer to Hertz than the Giants are to the Bears.

Linebacker Lawrence Taylor, the greatest Giant, left kicking and screaming like a little kid and had to be calmed on the sideline by coach Bill Parcells. The Bears ran at him, cut him down and picked on him until all he could do was cuss like an All-Pro.

The Bears offensive line did not allow a sack against a Giants' rush that had led the league in sacks. The offense also had no penalties or turnovers.

"Our players had a mission," said coach Mike Ditka. "The defense, you gotta love 'em. The job Buddy did was just a great job of coaching.

"It wasn't easy," Ditka insisted. "Nothing is easy in life. We beat a good football team. They manhandled the 49ers."

The Bears not only manhandled the Giants, they confused them like a bully who taps one shoulder and then sneaks up behind the other.

Ryan used what he called a "Smurf 46" with Gayle subbing for Perry. Ryan figured Gayle would match up better against the Giants' small third wide receiver, Phil McConkey, than linebackers Wilber Marshall or Otis Wilson.

Marshall and Wilson then split to either side of the Giants' line

instead of ganging up on one side as common in the "46." This put Wilson in Dent's usual spot over the weak-side tackle and put Dent over a guard where the Giants had trouble finding him and stopping the Bears' stunts.

Ryan had Wilson, Dent, Dan Hampton, Steve McMichael and Marshall—the Bears' five best pass rushers—going after Simms.

"They didn't know who to block," said Marshall. "That's what makes this defense so exciting, because it's so complicated nobody can figure it out."

Marshall, Duerson and middle linebacker Mike Singletary blitzed or faked blitzes to keep the Giants' backs in to block instead of swinging out for passes.

Simms took a page from the Miami Dolphins' playbook and rolled out, but his passes were hurried and off the mark.

If a 5-yard punt return for a touchdown wasn't a record, it was yet another way to entertain. Punter Sean Landeta was at his goal line because Dent had sacked Simms at the 12. Landeta said the 13-mile-an-hour wind blew the ball off course as he dropped it and it grazed off the side of his foot. It rolled to the side and was recorded as a punt for minus-7 yards.

Gayle managed to keep from laughing, scooped up the ball at the 5 and became the 22nd Bear and 9th defender to score a point in a season in which everybody has been a hero.

"I saw him graze the ball, so I knew it was a punt," said Gayle. "My first touchdown since high school."

The Bears soon drove 83 yards only to watch Kevin Butler miss a 26-yard field goal, the first of three misses for the usually reliable Butler.

But the drive settled two

PLAYOFF1

things: Willie Gault was going to have to be double-teamed and the Bears could move the ball.

Gault caught two passes in the drive and three in the first half.

"I talked to Willie, and Mike [Ditka] told him himself, 'Hey, we're going to need you,'" said McMahon. "He came up with great catches. He set the tone early. Then the safety had a tendency to play a little bit toward Willie and that's why Dennis [McKinnon] was having a heyday."

Walter Payton ran for 93 yards and the Bears got 363, exactly 93 more than average against the Giants.

The Giants had a chance to score late in the half when they hit two big plays and were on the Bears' 2-yard line with 31 seconds left. But three straight incompletions, including a drop by Bobby Johnson, set up a 19-yard field-goal attempt by Eric Schubert. The ball hit the left upright and bounced back.

"When they missed that field goal, I knew we were going to come out the third quarter and move down the field," said center Jay Hilgenberg. "We were jacked up."

Butler missed a 38-yard field goal, but three plays later, the Bears had another chance from the New York 41.

On a third-down play from the 23, McKinnon took McMahon's pass away from Elvis Patterson in the corner of the end zone.

"That was our biggest offensive play," said Ditka. "I thought

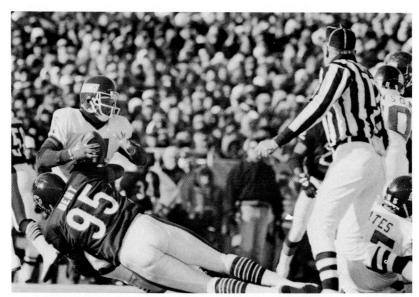

Defensive end Richard Dent lowers the boom on New York Giants' quarterback Phil Simms in the Bears' first playoff victory. Dent had 3½ sacks in a dominating individual performance. (Tribune photo by Charles Cherney)

Dan Hampton of the Bears gets up high enough to slap Giant quarterback Phil Simms' pass right back at him in the Bears' 21–0 victory in the NFC semifinals. (Tribune photo by Ed Wagner Jr.)

the seven points they would neutralize somewhere along the line, although they didn't."

Two series later, the Bears wrapped it up when McMahon connected on a 46-yard pass to tight end Tim Wrightman to set up the final touchdown.

From the 20, Ditka called a run, but McMahon saw a blitz, audibled and threw a perfect strike to McKinnon between Patterson and free safety Terry Kinard.

"They started stacking against the run and tried to free up Taylor by putting him over the center," said McMahon. "We had no way to block him, so we had to start going outside and start throwing the ball.

"Once we got the lead, I thought maybe they thought we would start running to control the clock, so it left their corners man-to-man on our wide receivers."

Nine of McMahon's 11 completions were against the wind. "It wasn't as big a factor as I thought it would be," said McMahon. "I threw better against the wind. Why? Who knows? Why'd I cut my hair this summer? I don't know."

"When the game is on the line and you've got to perform, he's the kind of guy who turns it on," said fullback Matt Suhey. "He has the mentality of a running back or an offensive lineman stuck in a quarterback body."

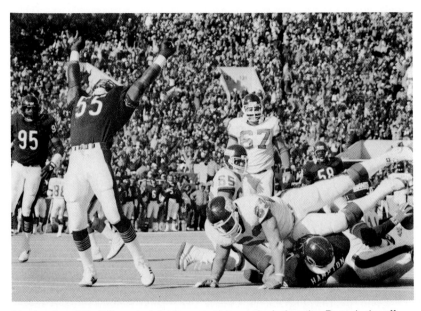

Linebacker Otis Wilson celebrates another sack during the Bears' playoff victory over the New York Giants. (Tribune photo by Bob Langer)

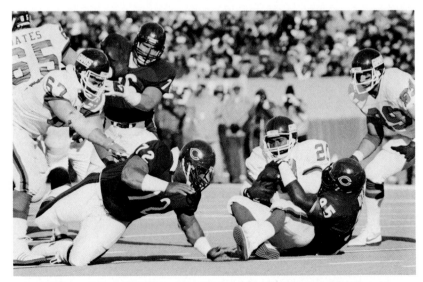

Richard Dent (95) and William Perry helped the Bears' defense shut down star running back Joe Morris (20) and his New York teammates Jan. 5. They did it again the following Sunday against Los Angeles, shutting out the Rams 24–0. (Tribune photo by Ed Wagner Jr.)

Superb Bears in Super Bowl

By Don Pierson

The Bears are in the Super Bowl.

Cut it out and paste it up. Roll it around your tongue. Say it once, twice, as many times as it takes to wrap it around your mind.

The Bears wrapped Eric Dickerson and the Los Angeles Rams around their big fingers Jan. 12 in a smashing 24–0 victory for the National Football Conference championship.

They left determined and favored to wrap Super Bowl rings around their fingers when they play the New England Patriots, the American Football Conference champions, Jan. 26 in New Orleans.

In a season full of one-upmanship, the shutout was one point better than the San Francisco 49ers' 23–0 victory over the Bears for the NFC title in January 1985. The Bears, who beat the New York Giants 21–0 on Jan. 5, will enter Super Bowl XX as the only team ever to record two straight playoff shutouts.

They wanted the Miami Dolphins again to erase the only blemish on their record. But the Patriots will serve the purpose for which the Bears seem destined.

In another subdued locker room where a few cigars were the only signs of a victory celebration, Ditka turned to Robert Frost for explanation and further inspiration.

"There's a poem that says something about we've come many miles but we've got many miles to go," said Ditka. "I don't want to sound like I'm not happy about what happened today, but we're on a mission and it won't be finished until we're finished in New Orleans."

The snow that started to swirl around Soldier Field late in the game was only confetti sprinkled by George Halas.

"He sent the sunshine, the snow, the touchdowns, everything," said Ditka.

A gusty 25-mile-an-hour wind blew only in the faces of the Rams and always at the backs of the Bears. It had to be a Windy City wind the way Bears' quarterback Jim McMahon threw only strikes and Rams' quarterback Dieter Brock threw only balls.

McMahon ran for one touchdown when he was supposed to pass and passed for another touchdown to Willie Gault when the Bears were supposed to run.

He threw against the wind and with the wind and through the wind in a performance marked by utter defiance from the time he substituted a headband that said "ROZELLE" for his outlawed adidas headband.

"You don't understand how well our quarterback threw the football," said Ditka of McMahon, who completed 16 of 25 passes for 164 yards.

McMahon's primary target was Walter Payton, who gained only 32 yards rushing but added 48 yards on 7 receptions. He also wore a ROZELLE headband instead of his ROOS headband that NFL commissioner Pete Rozelle doesn't like to see.

"Eleven years of climbing mountains and all the sweat finally paid off," said Payton. "I wish this was the Super Bowl."

The routinely awesome defense stuffed Dickerson from the first play, when free safety Gary Fencik moved to the line of scrimmage in another one of coordinator Buddy Ryan's unpredictable schemes.

Dickerson fumbled twice and the Bears recovered the second to set up the 22-yard touchdown pass to Gault that made it 17–0 in the third quarter.

McMahon called the play and executed it perfectly, rolling to his left and hitting the streaking Gault in the back corner of the end zone.

"The coach sent in a draw play I didn't agree with, so I called my own," said McMahon.

Ryan had predicted at least three fumbles by Dickerson.

"Only had two. If they would have run him more, he would have had three," said Ryan.

"Two out of three ain't bad," said William "the Refrigerator" Perry, who waved two fingers that looked suspiciously like a victory sign in Dickerson's face.

Dickerson carried only 17 times for 46 yards as the Rams were forced to let Brock play catch-up after the first 10 minutes, when the Bears took a 10–0 lead.

Brock looked like a man caught in a house of moving mirrors. The defense chased him until he finally coughed up the ball on a sack by Richard Dent and watched linebacker Wilber Marshall run 52 yards for the final touchdown.

It was a fitting punctuation for a defense that simply refuses to show mercy. Dan Hampton sat in the middle of the field and raised both arms over his head to hail the end of decades of frustration for a city and a franchise.

The celebration had started midway through the fourth quarter, with uncharacteristic hugs and smiles on the sideline and in the huddle. The crowd of 63,522 chanted "Super Bowl" and Ditka congratulated players one by one.

By the time it was over, the Bears were starting to get serious about their next stop, but not

PLAYOFF2

before Ditka told them he had never seen a defense dominate so totally.

"It was the first time we had seen glassy eyes," said safety Dave Duerson. "The Iron Guy softened up."

Nobody else did.

Defensive tackle Steve McMichael, still seething at Ryan for yanking him early in the fourth quarter to rest his ailing knees, snapped: "We've got to work our butts off for two weeks. Then it will be time to party for six months."

"I don't think we're ready for the season to end," said Hampton. "We still have a lot to prove. You don't see a lot of screaming and hollering and going crazy."

For Fencik, it was "a satisfying feeling. But this year we expected to win. It is different from previous years, when we were just here. Every week has reinforced our confidence. It's a matter of if we're playing the way we're capable of playing, we can beat anyone."

The fans might have been skeptical, but most of the Bears have never played on a losing team.

The Bears beat the Patriots 20–7 Sept. 15 in what the Bears consistently described as their absolute best defensive performance in a season in which they have held 13 of 18 opponents to 10 points or less.

The Patriots were in Bears' territory for a total of 21 seconds, including the 90-yard touchdown pass to Craig James that ruined the shutout late in the game.

Hampton was asked when the Bears gained control of the line of scrimmage against the Rams.

"Kickoff," he said.

By midway through the first quarter, Hampton could see defeat in the Rams' faces.

"I can tell by looking in their eyes whether they want to play or not. I knew they weren't really sure they wanted to be in Chicago playing us," said Hampton.

Fencik clapped when the Rams won the toss and elected to receive, a decision Rams' coach John Robinson said he regretted.

"I felt so confident our defense could put them in the hole," said Fencik.

When Kevin Butler kicked deep, high and away from Ron Brown and Bears' linebacker Cliff Thrift nailed Barry Redden at the 18, the Bears soon turned the field position into the 10–0 cushion.

On first down, Fencik nailed Dickerson for no gain in the hole and the tone was set.

Ryan had Fencik moving up from his deep weak safety spot and Duerson moving back at strong safety to confuse the Rams and keep them from running effectively to the weak side. Fencik ended up with seven solo tackles to tie middle linebacker Mike Singletary for the team lead.

The defense also used their regular "46" defense and a nickel and short-yardage alignment with tall Tyrone Keys substituting for Perry or Duerson. Keys batted down one of three passes the Bears tipped to keep Brock's 10-for-31 day miserable.

Ryan also threw in a "Jet" defense with linebackers Marshall, Singletary and Otis Wilson bunched in the middle.

"We beat New England about four or five years ago with that and used it a little bit against Detroit this year," said Ryan. "TCU used it to beat Oklahoma when I was coaching high school in Texas."

McMahon got the ball for the first time at his 44. A 20-yard pass to Emery Moorehead and a 19-yard pass to Gault got the Bears going. On third and 9, McMahon dropped back against

Jim McMahon (9) puts the finishing touches on his 16-yard touchdown run against the Rams by spiking the ball. Bearing witness to the authoritative effort—along with approving Chicago fans—is tight end Emery Moorehead (87). (Tribune photo by Bob Langer)

six defensive backs and ran 16 yards for the touchdown behind a block by Dennis Gentry.

Two bad passes by Brock and another stuff of Dickerson gave the Bears the ball at the Rams' 49.

McMahon hit Payton for 19 yards and Tim Wrightman and Gault for 13 more to get Butler in range for a 34-yard field goal.

There was still 4:26 left in the first quarter when the scoreboard flashed: "The Bears would like to thank all our fans for their support in the 1985 season."

The only thing missing was "Drive carefully."

The Rams' longest drive of the day was 27 yards on their final possession. On half of their 16 possessions, it was three downs and out. They averaged 2.2 yards a play.

The Bears stopped Dickerson by standing up his blockers and waiting for Dickerson to commit. Then they hit him before he could hit a gap.

Dickerson's fumble, which was caused by Wilson and recovered by Richardson early in the third quarter, set up McMahon at his 48. Again he took advantage of the field position. He threw a perfect pass to Gault on one third down, and when Ditka decided to go for it on fourth and 6 from the 35, McMahon rolled out and fired a 13-yard strike to Payton.

"They were putting good pressure in the pocket, so we went with the sprintout," said McMahon.

It put the ball on the 22. On second down, McMahon nixed Ditka's call for a draw and found Gault ahead of cornerback LeRoy Irvin. Gault had run a corner route after faking inside.

"He thought I was going to cut across the field, but I didn't," said Gault.

"Biggest play of the game," said McMahon.

"The way we were playing defense, it didn't matter what we scored," said Ditka.

"I'm so happy for the fans who sat out on a lot of cold days when we weren't so fun to watch," said Singletary.

"We don't mean to cause no trouble. We're just doing the 'Super Bowl Shuffle,' " said Fencik.

The heck they don't cause trouble. How is a Dixieland band going to play the 'Super Bowl Shuffle'?

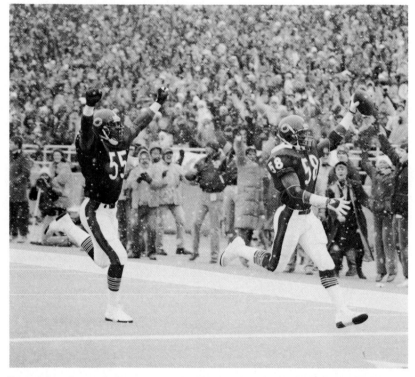

Bears' fans knew their team was headed to the Super Bowl when Wilber Marshall (58) recovered a fumble and returned it for the final touchdown against the Los Angeles Rams. Following Marshall as he steams into the end zone after a 52-yard run is an emotional Otis Wilson. (Tribune photo by Bob Langer)

Bears bury all the 'wait untils'

By John Kass

A generation's worth of empty boasts and broken promises by Chicago sports teams that have turned the city's fans into shrugging fatalists were finally burned away on a windy Jan. 12 as the Chicago Bears made good.

The 24–0 beating administered to the Los Angeles Rams at Soldier Field put the Bears into their first Super Bowl, against the New England Patriots in New Orleans for the National Football League championship.

Minutes after the victory, the game scene was being remembered by some who mentally superimposed the image of George Halas's ghost over the stadium packed with 63,522 shouting and barking fans.

But some diehard fans also remember the bad years: when the team had quarterbacks who could talk better than they could throw, five-and-dime backfields, and when in 1969 the Bears were 1–13, tied as the worst team in football only to lose the coin flip to the Pittsburgh Steelers for quarterback Terry Bradshaw, the first choice in the college draft that year.

Near the end of the NFC title game, when the snow, as promised, finally began to fall on the Rams' slumping shoulders, what Bears' fan in Soldier Field, or in taverns or homes, did not flinch at the mention of the recent ugly and choking betrayals of the city by the Cubs and White Sox?

"I got a friend who couldn't take it no more," said Robert Neil, a retired U.S. Army sergeant, as he drank a celebratory beer in a restaurant in the Gage Park neighborhood on the Southwest Side. "The Cubs broke his heart and so did the Sox. Now he

Jim McMahon (9) congratulates Walter Payton on a job well done after the Bears had shut out Atlanta. McMahon didn't play in the Falcon game because of tendinitis in his right shoulder. (Tribune photo by Charles Cherney)

hates 'em. *Hates 'em.* I told him not to be afraid about the Bears. They won't choke. They won in 1963 and they'd do it again.

"I told him that they'd win, but he wouldn't listen. So I got mad and I said, 'Hey, you don't come by me no more when they do win. You'll wake up. Sometime before you're dead, you'll say the Bears were good and I was too afraid and I missed it all.'"

Since the collapse of the 1969 Cubs—another front-running team that was anointed the me-

dia and advertising darling until it rolled on its back during the infamous National League pennant race—many Chicago fans have never quite been able to draw deep breaths under pressure. Not even the Sting's 1984 Soccer Bowl title did much to soothe their feelings.

That fear of failure for some fans, and the harping whine inherent in the city's adopted credo of "Wait 'til next year," caused some Chicagoans to become angry when some Bears' players began to sing the "Super Bowl Shuffle" and lend their bodies to television commercials before the team reached the Super Bowl.

But as the Bears secured the league's conference crown, the fans were finally rewarded with the city's first football title since the 1963 Bears won the NFL championship at Wrigley Field.

"At the end of the game, I pinched myself to see if it was true," said South Sider Frank Nawta. "If you're from Chicago, you know disaster lurks around the corner."

Predictably, Rush Street became the site of impromptu parades as cars honked horns and people decorated in orange and blue waved to strangers and began to celebrate seriously. Similar behavior also was seen in the city's neighborhoods, where the taverns were full and the Rams were hanged in effigy from several roofs of two-flat buildings.

Al Sord, proprietor of the Candlelight Lodge, a restaurant in the Gage Park neighborhood, fed his waitresses and busboys roast chicken and potatoes and told them to forget about working during the game. They all sat at the bar and watched with other neighbors in the lounge as the restaurant tables remained empty.

EPILOGUE

"We're all family for one thing," Sord said. "And we won't get anybody in for dinner, not today. Nobody will sit down in a restaurant and miss this. I don't even want people to ask me for drinks unless there's a commercial."

At the end of the bar, Neil and a friend, Tony Shalton, planned a Super Bowl victory party—in Shalton's back yard, for July 4, 1986.

"I've got the Ram game taped and in the bag," Shalton said. "They'll win the next one and we'll get a big screen TV, put it in the back yard and party when everybody else is watching baseball."

Outside Soldier Field before the L.A. game, as the anxiety of each fan seemed to multiply and gnaw at the crowd walking into the stadium, the pregame ritual for two working boys was already over.

The two self-described "businessmen" had begun warming up eight hours before the Bears and the Rams rolled out of their hotel beds and hoped that their efforts would pay off.

At 3:30 a.m., Kali Bussell and his cousin, Jerry Glover, awoke in their South Chicago apartments, ate bowls of cold cereal and then traveled to 18th Street and Calumet Avenue to sell Chicago Bear souvenirs to fans who paid handsomely for the privilege of stepping inside the stadium.

There, in the predawn cold, the two boys staked out their territory, rolled up a wad of dollar bills and tried to keep warm as Bear fans—wrapped in everything from snowmobile suits and furs to electric heating pads—crossed in front of them and over the footbridge that spans the railroad tracks to Soldier Field.

"I'm a businessman more than a Bear fan," said Kali, a 6th grader at Avalon Park School. "I'm gonna make a lot of money today; so let's hope they win. But I'm not gonna waste it on women. I'm single, but you never know what happens when a man's got money."

A block away, two Chicago police officers sat sullenly in their squad car, smoking cigars and complaining that rank has its privileges.

The two officers sat listening to their police radio with no hope of watching the game. Each time a squad car with a superior passed by, they smirked.

"All the brass check up on us so that we're not watching the game on a little TV, but they've got their own," one said. "They've got their radios, they've got their TVs, and here we are like hungry men just able to watch people going to have fun. It's cruel, isn't it?"

But the victory was ever-so-sweet. Doubt is a constant emotion of Chicago sports fans. Even that began to vanish as it became clear the Bears would win, convincingly.

The Bears' wondrous season has been dissected and analyzed each week by self-proclaimed aficionados and by relative newcomers drawn to the game by the

The Bears, who used to complain about a lack of vocal support from their Soldier Field fans, found the noise level mounting with their victory total this season. (Tribune photo by Charles Cherney)

heat generated by a winner and the national celebrity status of some of the players.

On a Chinatown street outside the grocery, Fong Chung Ping had difficulty in expressing himself about the game. In response to many questions about the mythology of football, its impact on Chicago and the general emotional health of the city, the man smiled, jumped up and down and punched his fists together.

"Football? I like it," he said. "Fridge. Fridge. You go now. Watch TV."

Quarterback Jim McMahon (left) and tackle Jimbo Covert recreate a familiar scene on the Bears: congratulating Walter Payton. (Tribune photo by Bob Langer)

1985–86 Chicago Bears Scrapbook

Brad Anderson 86

Wide receiver Arizona
Height—6-2 Weight—198
Born—1-21-61,
Glendale, Ariz.
Acquisition — Selected in the eighth round [212th player] of the '84 draft.
1985 season — Appeared in 15 games and started none . . . Finished the preseason with best per-catch average [29.0] among wide receivers . . . Plays a lot on special teams.
Pro career — Made two starts and appeared in 13 games and both playoff games as a rookie in 1984 . . . Caught a 49-yard TD pass from Jim McMahon at Tampa Bay [10-21-84] and earned the game ball.

Tom Andrews 60

Tackle/center Louisville
Height—6-4 Weight—267
Born—1-11-62,
Parma, Ohio
Acquisition — Selected in the fourth round [98th player] of the 1984 draft.
1985 season — Played in 13 games and started none . . . Waived after the third preseason game and re-signed 9-5 . . . Primarily a substitute in the offensive line and a member of the special teams.
Pro career — In his second year . . . Played in seven games and both postseason contests in 1984 . . . Drafted as a tackle but used as a back-up center to Jay Hilgenberg.

Brian Baschnagel 84

Wide receiver Ohio State
Height—6-0 Weight—193
Born—1-8-54,
Kingston, N.Y.
Acquisition — Third-round draft choice in 1976.
1985 season — On injured reserve all season.
Pro career — Fourteenth on the team's all-time receiving list in catches [134] and 12th on the all-time receiving list in yardage [2,024].

Kurt Becker 79

Guard Michigan
Height—6-5 Weight—267
Born—12-22-58,
Aurora, Ill.
Acquisition — Sixth-round draft choice in 1982.
1985 season — Started the first three games before being placed on injured reserve because of surgery on his right knee 10-1.
Pro career — In his fourth year . . . Steady performer at right guard, where he was a season-long starter in 1984 . . . Earned a game ball vs. New Orleans in 1984 after Payton broke Jim Brown's NFL rushing record.

Mark Bortz 62

Guard Iowa
Height—6-6 Weight—269
Born—2-12-61,
Pardeeville, Wis.
Acquisition — Second choice in the eighth round of the 1983 draft.
1985 season — Received a game ball for his performance vs. San Francisco [10-13] . . . Started every game.
Pro career — In his third year . . . Has played in 46 of 47 games since joining the club in '83 . . . Started 15 of 16 games and both playoff games at left guard in '84–85 . . . Played extremely well against Dallas's Randy White [9-30-84] . . . Earned a game ball vs. New Orleans when Payton broke the NFL rushing record . . . Has a bright future as an offensive lineman after being switched from defense as rookie.

Maury Buford 8

Punter Texas Tech
Height—6-0 Weight—191
Born—2-18-60,
Mt. Pleasant, Tex.
Acquisition — From San Diego 8-20 in exchange for a conditional draft choice in 1986.
1985 season — Received a game ball vs. Green Bay 10-21 . . . Five punts of 60-plus yards.
Pro career — In his fourth season . . . Top punter in San Diego history with a career 42.7-yard average . . . Third in the NFL in 1983 with a 43.9-yard average.

Kevin Butler 6

Placekicker Georgia
Height—6-1 Weight—190
Born—7-24-62,
Savannah, Ga.
Acquisition — Fourth-round selection in the 1985 draft [105th player].
1985 season — Set a Bear scoring record with 144 points . . . Set an NFL record for most points scored by a rookie . . . Forty-six yard FG against Dallas 11-17 was his longest of the season.

Brian Cabral 54

Linebacker Colorado
Height—6-1 Weight—227
Born—6-23-56,
Ft. Benning, Ga.
Acquisition — Signed as a free agent 9-1-81.
1985 season — Played in one game and started none . . . Was placed on the injured reserve list after undergoing knee surgery to repair torn cartilage.
Pro career — Valuable special teamer who appeared in every game in '84 . . . Fourth in special team tackles.

Jim Covert 74

Off. tackle Pittsburgh
Height—6-4 Weight—271

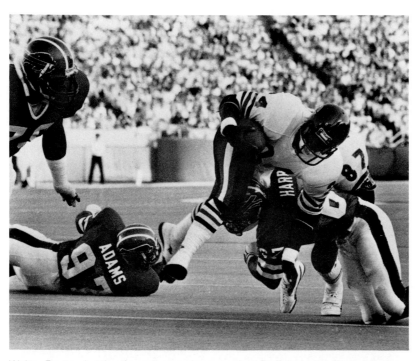

Walter Payton battles for extra yardage against Buffalo in the Bears' final preseason game. Payton went on to gain 1,551 yards during the regular season. (Tribune photo by Bob Langer)

Willie Gault attempts to display concentration at full speed as he is pushed by a San Francisco defender. (Tribune photo by Charles Cherney)

Born—3-22-60,
Conway, Pa.
Acquisition — First-round selection in 1983 draft.
1985 season — Pro Bowl selection . . . Had a streak of 35 consecutive starts snapped vs. Washington . . . Started the other 15 games.
Pro career — In his third year, he's the youngest captain in the NFL . . . Earned a game ball vs. New Orleans [10-7] . . . Consensus all-rookie selection [Football Digest, UPI, Pro Football Weekly].

Richard Dent 95

Defensive end   Tenn. State
Height—6-5   Weight—253
Born—12-13-60,
Atlanta, Ga.
Acquisition — First selection in the eighth round of the 1983 draft.
1985 season — Led team with 17 sacks . . . Had 1-yard interception for touchdown vs. Dallas 11-17 . . . 38 tackles . . . Selected to NFC Pro Bowl team.
Pro career — Made his first Pro Bowl appearance in 1984 as a starter . . . 3 sacks in Pro Bowl . . . Earned numerous post-season honors: College and Pro Football Weekly's 1st team, All-NFC, AP second team, UPI 1st team . . . Led the NFC in sacks in '84 with 17½ and established a club record for sacks.

Dave Duerson 22

Safety   Notre Dame
Height—6-1   Weight—203
Born—11-28-60,
Muncie, Ind.
Acquisition — Third-round draft choice in 1983.
1985 season — Made the NFC Pro Bowl team . . . Earned a game ball vs. Detroit 11-10 . . . 5 interceptions, 64 tackles and 2 sacks.
Pro career — Led the club in special team tackles in '84 . . . Earned a game ball at Green Bay [9-16-84] and vs. the Raiders [11-4-84].

Pat Dunsmore 88

Tight end   Drake
Height—6-3   Weight—237
Born—10-2-59,
Duluth, Minn.
Acquisition — Fourth-round

choice in the 1983 draft.
1985 season — On injured reserve all season.
Pro career — Alternated with Emery Moorehead as a play messenger in '84 . . . Caught first career TD pass vs. Detroit [11-18-84] . . . Caught a 19-yard TD pass from Payton in the Bears' 23–19 playoff victory over the Redskins . . . Played in all 16 games in '83 . . . Had the best game of his career vs. Detroit [10-16-83] when he caught 5 passes for 73 yards.

Gary Fencik 45

Safety   Yale
Height—6-1   Weight—196
Born—6-11-54, Chicago
Acquisition — Signed as free agent 9-15-76.
1985 season — His 118 tackles led the team . . . Also had 5 interceptions . . . His 949 career tackles are second only to Dick Butkus in Bear history . . . Recorded his 35th career interception vs. Atlanta [11-17] to become second on the all-time Bear list behind Richie Petitbon [37].
Pro career — In 1984, had two interceptions in the season opener vs. Tampa, including a 61-yard return . . . Also picked off two Joe Montana passes in the playoff at S.F. [1-6-85] . . . Had two interceptions vs. the L.A. Raiders [11-4-84] . . . Finished second on the team in tackles with 103 and first in solos with 82 . . . Earned NFC Defensive Player of the Week honors vs. Tampa Bay [9-2-84] . . . Turned in a nine-tackle performance vs. Green Bay [12-9-84] . . . In 1983, he missed eight games with a groin injury . . . Named all-NFL by Pro Football Weekly in '82 . . . Consensus all-pro in '81 . . . Voted to the NFC Pro Bowl squad for the second time after the '81 season, first time as starter . . . Scored his first NFL touchdown with a 69-yard interception return vs. the Broncos [12-20-81] . . . All-pro in '79 when he had six interceptions . . . Owns seven game ball trophies.

Jeff Fisher 24

Def. back   Southern Cal
Height—5-11   Weight—195
Born—2-25-58,
Culver City, Calif.
Acquisition — Seventh-round

draft choice in 1981.
1985 season — On injured reserve all season.
Pro career — In 1984, became the Bears all-time leading punt returner with 123 . . . Suffered a broken leg in '83 and missed the final eight games . . . His 88-yard punt return for a TD vs. the Bucs [9-20-81] was the longest by a Bear in Soldier Field.

Leslie Frazier 21

Cornerback   Alcorn State
Height—6-0   Weight—187
Born—4-3-59,
Columbus, Miss.
Acquisition — Signed as a free agent 7-18-81.
1985 season — Led team with six interceptions . . . Had a 29-yard interception return for a TD vs. Tampa Bay [9-8] . . . 52 tackles.
Pro career — In 1984, a foot injury caused him to miss five games . . . Earned a game ball vs. Denver [9-9-84] . . . Led the team in '83 in passes defended [21].

Andy Frederick 71

Off. tackle   New Mexico
Height—6-6   Weight—265
Born—7-25-54, Oak Park
Acquisition — From Browns in a trade 4-28-83.
1985 season — Started at left tackle for injured Jim Covert against Washington.
Pro career — Game ball vs. Saints [10-7-84] as part of the line on record-breaking day for Payton . . . Fifth-round draft choice by the Cowboys in '77.

Steve Fuller 4

Quarterback   Clemson
Height—6-4   Weight—195
Born—1-5-57, Enid, Okla.
Acquisition — From Rams for two draft choices.
1985 season — Ran for three touchdowns . . . Bears 3–1 in games he started.
Pro career — Led the Bears to the '84 NFC title game after Jim McMahon's injury . . . Relieved McMahon vs. the Raiders [11-4] and completed 4 of 5 passes in a 17–6 victory . . . Rated as the NFL's top passer in the next four games . . . Chiefs second choice in first round of '79 draft.

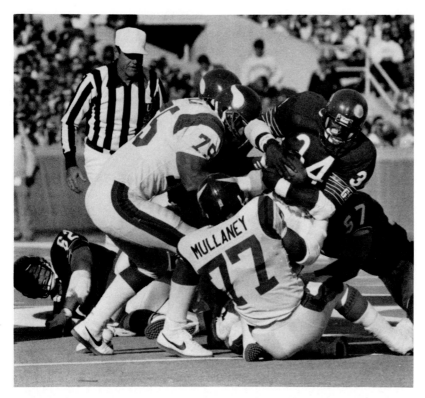

Walter Payton struggles for a few of his 118 yards against the Vikings at Soldier Field. (Tribune photo by Ed Wagner Jr.)

Tackle Steve McMichael, the Bears' most consistent defensive lineman much of the season, forces Green Bay quarterback Jim Zorn to throw off the mark in a Nov. 3 game. The Bears rallied to win 16–10 after McMichael tackled Zorn in the end zone for a safety. (Tribune photo by Bob Langer)

Willie Gault 83

Wide receiver Tennessee
Height—6-0 Weight—178
Born—9-5-60,
Griffin, Ga.
Acquisition — Second selection in the first round of the 1983 draft.
1985 season — Had a 99-yard kickoff return for a TD vs. Washington . . . Had his best day in the NFL vs. Vikings [9-19] with 6 pass receptions for 146 yards and a TD.
Pro career — Led team in TD receptions [6] and yards per catch [17.3] in '84 . . . His 40 receptions in '83 were the most by a Bears rookie since Harlon Hill caught 45 in '54.

Shaun Gayle 23

Cornerback Ohio State
Height—5-11 Weight—193
Born—3-8-62,
Hampton, Va.
Acquisition — Selected in the 10th round of the '84 draft.
1985 season — Blocked a punt that led to a TD in a 38–28 victory vs. Bucs in the season opener . . . 18 tackles.
Pro career — Emerged as the third cornerback in '84 and started 6 games . . . Recorded his only interception of season in his first NFL start at St. Louis [10-14-84].

Dennis Gentry 29

Running back Baylor
Height—5-8 Weight—181
Born—2-10-59,
Lubbock, Tex.
Acquisition — Selected in the fourth round of the 1982 draft [89th player].
1985 season — Had a 94-yard run kickoff return for a touchdown vs. Lions [12-22].
Pro career — Scored his first NFL touchdown at Tampa Bay [10-21-84].

Dan Hampton 99

Defensive tackle Arkansas
Height—6-5 Weight—267
Born—1-19-57,
Oklahoma City
Acquisition — First selection in the first round of the '79 draft.
1985 season — Had a tipped pass vs. Dallas that was caught by Richard Dent for a 1-yard touch-down . . . Pro Bowl selection for the fourth time . . . Shifted to left end for the last eight games . . . Came back from off-season knee surgery.
Pro career — Named to Sporting News, PFW, AP and NEA all-pro first teams in 1984 . . . Third on the team in sacks [11.5 for 95.5 yards] and 6th in tackles [54] . . . His 1984 high was two sacks vs. St. Louis [10-14-84] and Detroit [12-16-84] . . . Had 2 sacks [for minus 19 yds.] in the playoffs . . . His 8 tackles vs. Green Bay [12-9-84] was also his best of the season . . . Started 11 games in '83 because of injuries but still finished 4th on the team in sacks with 5 . . . Selected to several all-pro teams following the '82 season; Pro Football Weekly named him the NFL's most valuable player . . . Led the Bears in sacks in '82 with 7 and was second in tackles with 71 while starting all 9 games at right end . . . Led the team in sacks [11.5] and the defensive line in tackles [73] in '80 . . . Made his first pro sack on former Buc Doug Williams as rookie . . . First rookie to start on the Bears' defense since '75 . . . Selected in the '79 draft behind LB Tom Cousineau [Browns], DT Mike Bell [Chiefs] and QB Jack Thompson [Bengals] . . . Bears obtained that pick plus TE Bobby Moore from Tampa Bay for DE Wally Chambers . . . Voted '79 Brian Piccolo Award by veterans.

Mike Hartenstine 73

Def. end Penn State
Height—6-3 Weight—254
Born—7-27-53,
Allentown, Pa.
Acquisition — Second-round draft choice in 1975.
1985 season — His fumble recovery set up a score vs. Atlanta [11-24] . . . 19 tackles and 1 sack.
Pro career — Received game balls in '84 for both Tampa Bay games . . . Led the team in sacks in '83 with 12.

Jay Hilgenberg 63

Center Iowa
Height—6-3 Weight—258
Born—3-21-59,
Iowa City, Ia.
Acquisition — Signed as a free agent 5-8-81.
1985 season — Pro Bowl selection . . . Played in all 71 games since he joined the team in '81 . . . Started the last 38 games.
Pro career — Emerged as one of league's most consistent centers in his first year as a full-time starter in '84.

Stefan Humphries 75

Guard Michigan
Height—6-3 Weight—263
Born—1-20-62,
Broward, Fla.
Acquisition — Selected in third round of '84 draft.
1985 season — Was on injured reserve until he was brought back when Kurt Becker was injured.
Pro career — Played in 12 of the first 14 games in '84 before he was placed on injured reserve with a knee injury.

Tyrone Keys 98

Def. end Mississippi
Height—6-7 Weight—267
Born—10-24-59,
Brookhaven, Miss.
Acquisition — From the New York Jets for a 5th round draft choice in 1985 [7-13-83].
1985 season — Blocked a field goal vs. Green Bay . . . 9 tackles, 2 sacks.
Pro career — A valuable lineman who can play tackle or end . . . First NFL start was against the L.A. Rams; he made 7 tackles and knocked down a pass [11-6-83] . . . Played for British Columbia in Canada, '81–82.

Mitch Krenk 89

Tight end Nebraska
Height—6-2 Weight—233
Born—11-19-59,
Crete, Neb.
Acquisition — Claimed on waivers from Dallas 8-28-84.
1985 season — Spent season on injured reserve.
Pro career — Played in 10 games in '84, including both playoff games . . . Had 2 catches for 31 yards, including a 24-yard catch at San Diego [12-3-84].

Defenders Otis Wilson (55), Mike Singletary (50), Wilber Marshall (58), Richard Dent (95) and William Perry (72) surround Packer running back Eddie Lee Ivery in a 16–10 victory over the Packers Nov. 3. (Tribune photo by Bob Langer)

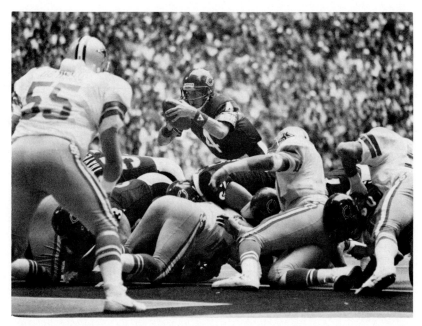

Quarterback Steve Fuller (4) dives in from the 1-yard line during the Bears' 44–0 rout of the Dallas Cowboys. (Tribune photo by Bob Langer)

James Maness 81

Receiver Tex. Christian
Height—6-1 Weight—174
Born—5-1-63,
Decatur, Tex.
Acquisition — Third-round selection in 1985 draft.
1985 season — Made his only catch, for 34 yards, vs. the Vikings [10-28] . . . Placed on injured reserve before the Detroit game [11-10].

Ken Margerum 82

Wide receiver Stanford
Height—6-0 Weight—180
Born—10-5-58,
Fountain Valley, Calif.
Acquisition — Third round of '81 draft [67th player].
1985 season — Played his best game of the year vs. Miami with 4 catches for 61 yards and 1 touchdown.
Pro career — Spent all of '84 on the physically unable to perform list after he tore the anterior cruciate ligament in his left knee during mini-camp . . . Had corrective surgery 5-24-84 . . . Named to PFWA, UPI, PFW all-rookie teams.

Wilber Marshall 58

Linebacker Florida
Height—6-1 Weight—225
Born—4-18-62,
Titusville, Fla.
Acquisition — 1st round draft choice [11th player] in '84 draft.
1985 season — Had best day as pro vs. Vikings, with his first interception and a recovered fumble late in 4th quarter . . . No. 3 tackler on the team with 78 . . . Also, 6 sacks and 5 interceptions.
Pro career — Made his first NFL start vs. Dallas [9-30-84] and made 8 tackles.

Dennis McKinnon 85

Wide receiver Florida St.
Height—6-1 Weight—185
Born—8-22-61,
Quitman, Ga.
Acquisition — Signed as free agent 5-4-83.
1985 season — Led the team with seven touchdown catches . . .

Bears are 13–0 in games in which McKinnon has caught a TD pass . . . Had his best day as a pro with 4 catches for 133 yards and 2 TDs against Minnesota [9-19].
Pro career — Started the first 12 games in '84 before missing the last four after arthroscopic surgery on left knee . . . Finished fourth in receptions [30] and third in yards [434] in '84 . . . Returned for the playoffs and played a key role in the victory over the Redskins with 4 catches for 72 yards and 1 TD . . . Received a game ball vs. New Orleans [10-7-84] . . . The team's leading punt returner in '83 [34 for 316] . . . Awarded a game ball at Philadelphia [10-23-83] after a 20-yard TD catch and five punt returns for 48 yards.

Jim McMahon 9

Quarterback
Brigham Young
Height—6-1 Weight—190
Born—8-21-59,
Jersey City, N.J.
Acquisition — No. 1 selection in the 1982 draft [5th player drafted].
1985 season — Came off the bench from an injured neck and leg to beat the Vikings 33–24 . . . Bears have won 23 of the last 27 games he has started . . . Caught a TD pass against Washington [9-29], the second of his career . . . Missed three straight starts because of tendinitis in the shoulder.
Pro career — An injury-plagued '84 season forced him to miss seven games and the playoffs . . . Was voted NFC Rookie of the Year by UPI in '82 . . . Brian Piccolo Award winner.

Steve McMichael 76

Defensive tackle Texas
Height—6-2 Weight—260
Born—10-17-57,
Houston, Tex.
Acquisition — Signed as a free agent 10-15-81.
1985 season — Tackled Eric Zorn in the end zone to lead a comeback over the Packers [11-3] . . . 44 tackles and 8 sacks . . . 38 consecutive starts.
Pro career — Started all season in '84 despite knee problems . . .

Third on the team in sacks [10] and 7th in tackles [42] in '84 . . . Named NFC Defensive Player of Week at Detroit [12-16-84] after recording 5 tackles and 2.5 sacks . . . Second on the team in sacks in '83 with 8.5 . . . Had a 64-yard run with a fumble vs. Bucs [1-2-83] . . . Joined the Bears after he was waived by the Patriots during '81 training camp . . . New England's 3rd round selection in '80.

Emery Moorehead 87

Tight end Colorado
Height—6-2 Weight—225
Born—3-22-54,
Evanston, Ill.
Acquisition — Signed as a free agent 10-21-81.
1985 season — Recorded his NFL bests in catches [8] and yards [114] vs. Tampa Bay [10-6] . . . Bears' No. 2 receiver with 35 catches.
Pro career — Emerged as starter at midseason of 1984 and held the job through the playoffs . . . Earned game balls against Detroit [11-18-84] and Minnesota [10-28-84] . . . Caught a 13-yard TD pass from Fuller in the division-clinching victory over the Vikings [11-25-84] . . . Led the Bears in receiving yardage in '82 with 363, while starting every game . . . His five TD receptions in '82 were the most by a Bears' tight end since Ditka had five in '65 . . . Giants' 6th-round draft choice in '77.

Jim Morrissey 51

Linebacker Michigan State
Height—6-3 Weight—215
Born—12-24-62,
Flint, Mich.
Acquisition — Selected in the 11th round of the 1985 draft.
1985 season — Waived 9-2 and re-signed 9-10 after the Bears placed Brian Cabral on injured reserve . . . Valuable special teamer . . . 12 tackles.

Keith Ortego 96

Wide receiver McNeese State
Height—6-0 Weight—180
Born—8-30-63
Acquisition — Free agent, signed 5-14-85.
1985 season — Played in seven

Mike Richardson, escorted by tackle Steve McMichael (76) and fellow linebacker Wilber Marshall (58), motors toward the end zone for a touchdown after intercepting a pass by Cowboy quarterback Gary Hogeboom. (Tribune photo by Ed Wagner Jr.)

Willie Gault, breaking away from Atlanta cornerback Bobby Butler, caught only one touchdown pass in the regular season and one in the playoffs, but the threat of his speed stretched enemy defenses. (Tribune photo by Bob Langer)

games since coming off injured reserve ... Had arthroscopic knee surgery in training camp ... Returned 17 punts for 158 yards and a 9.3 average.

Walter Payton 34

Running back Jackson State
Height—5-11 Weight—202
Born—7-25-54,
Columbia, Miss.
Acquisition — No. 1 selection in the 1975 draft.
1985 season — Had 9 consecutive 100-yard games to set an NFL record ... Became the Bears' leading scorer with 648 points, surpassing Bob Thomas ... Selected to the Pro Bowl for the 8th time ... Had 192 yards against Green Bay [11-3] ... Had 10 100-yard games ... 152 straight starts ... NFC player of the month for October.
Pro career — Became NFL's all-time leading rusher vs. New Orleans [10-7-84], surpassing Jim Brown. Accomplished the feat with 154-yard effort. The record-breaking run came in the third quarter [6 yards]. He broke it in his 10th season on his 2,795th NFL rushing attempt ... Also broke Brown's combined yardage mark vs. Broncos [9-9-84] with a 179-yard effort ... Broke Bears' mark for career receptions in '84 ... Played QB for four plays vs. Packers [12-9-84] ... Threw two TD passes to Matt Suhey on the halfback option in '84 ... Broke Brown's record for most 100-yard games [58] ... Owns the NFL single-game rushing record of 275 yards vs. Vikings [11-20-77] ... Took an unprecedented 5th consecutive NFC rushing title in '80 with 1,460 yards ... Youngest player to be voted NFL MVP at 23 in '77 ... Won the '75 kickoff return title with an average of 31.7 ... Owns the Pro Bowl record for most rushing attempts in a career, surpassing O. J. Simpson.

William Perry 72

Def. tackle Clemson
Height—6-2 Weight—318
Born—12-16-62,
Aiken, S.C.
Acquisition — 1st-round selection in the '85 draft [22nd player].
1985 season — Became a nation-al phenomenon by scoring his first NFL touchdown vs. the Packers [10-21] ... Blocked for Walter Payton's 2 TDs in the same game ... Carried 5 times for 7 yards and 2 TDs and caught a TD pass ... Started the last eight games at defensive tackle ... 31 tackles, 5 sacks.

Reggie Phillips 48

Cornerback Southern Methodist
Height—5-10 Weight—170
Born—12-20-60,
Houston, Tex.
Acquisition — Second-round selection in the 1985 draft [49th player].
1985 season — Recovered a fumble late in the fourth quarter vs. the Pats 9-15 to help preserve a Bear victory ... Made his first career start vs. Detroit [11-10] ... 10 tackles.

Dan Rains 53

Linebacker Cincinnati
Height—6-1 Weight—229
Born—4-26-56,
Rochester, Pa.
Acquisition — Signed as a free agent 5-14-82.
1985 season — On injured reserve all season.
Pro career — Valued special teamer in '84 ... Started 5 games in '83 ... Has forced 2 fumbles and recovered 1 for the Bears ... Career stats show 32 tackles, with a high of 25 in '83 ... Discovered in film of '81 semipro game.

Joe Rammuno 67

Off. lineman Wyoming
Height—6-3 Weight—265
Born—2-1-62,
Steamboat Springs, Colo.
Acquisition — Signed as a free agent 5-8-85.
1985 season — On injured reserve all season.

Mike Richardson 27

Cornerback Ariz. State
Height—6-0 Weight—188
Born—5-23-61,
Compton, Calif.
Acquisition — Selected in the second round of the 1983 draft.
1985 season — His 36-yard inter-ception return for a TD was his first in the NFL; it put the Bears ahead 17–0 vs. Dallas [11-17] ... Earned game balls vs. Atlanta and Washington ... Has four interceptions, 41 tackles.
Pro career — Led the team in passes defended with 13 in '84 ... Knocked down three passes in his pro debut vs. Falcons [9-4-83] ... Awarded a game ball vs. Philadelphia [9-23-83] after 5 tackles and 2 passes defended.

Ron Rivera 59

Linebacker California
Height—6-3 Weight—239
Born—1-7-62,
Monterey, Calif.
Acquisition — Picked in second round of '84 draft.
1985 season — Had a five-yard fumble return vs. the Lions for a touchdown ... 14 tackles, 5 sacks.
Pro career — Employed primarily as a special teams player in '84 ... Played in the final 15 games after sitting out the opener ... Had six tackles as a rookie.

Thomas Sanders 20

Running back Texas A&M
Height—5-11 Weight—203
Born—1-4-62,
Giddings, Tex.
Acquisition — Ninth-round selection in the 1985 draft [246th player].
1985 season — Scored a touchdown vs. Falcons [11-24] ... Finished the preseason with 7 yards a carry, best among running backs.

Mike Singletary 50

Middle linebacker Baylor
Height—6-0 Weight—228
Born—10-9-58,
Houston, Tex.
Acquisition — Second-round selection in the 1981 draft.
1985 season — Pro Bowl selection for the third straight year ... Had his season high of 14 tackles vs. Green Bay [11-3] ... Won a game ball in that game ... Was the NFC defensive player of the week vs. New England with 7 tackles, 3 sacks and 1 interception ... The team's No. 2

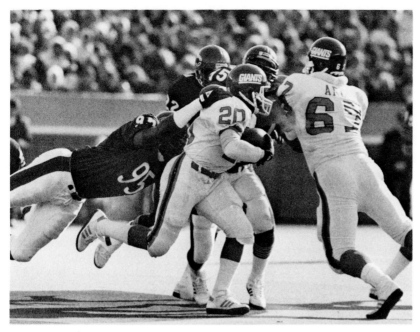

The Giants' Joe Morris was just one of the many running backs who felt the ominous presence of defensive end Richard Dent (95). The Chicago defensive unit once again was devastating as the Bears blanked the Giants 21–0 on Jan. 5 in the NFC semifinal game. (Tribune photo by Ed Wagner Jr.)

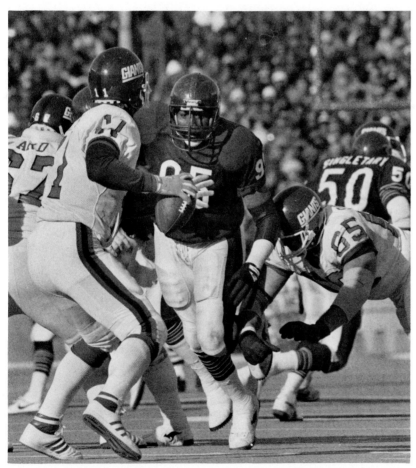

Defensive end Richard Dent seemed to spend a good deal of his time bearing down on the opposing quarterback, as the Giants' Phil Simms found out in the playoffs. (Tribune photo by Bob Langer)

tackler with 113 . . . Also has three sacks and one interception.

Pro career — First-team all-NFL choice by Sporting News, PFW, Football Digest, AP, NEA, PFWA. All-NFC by UPI in '84 . . . Led the Bears in tackles for the second consecutive year with 116, including 81 solos . . . Defensive captain and signal caller . . . Won a game ball in the '84 season opener vs. Tampa Bay [9-2] when he had interception and five tackles . . . Tied his NFL best with 3.5 sacks . . . Only linebacker to play in the Bears' "46" pass defense . . . Second on team with 3 forced fumbles in '84 . . . Led the team in tackles [148], solos [118], assists [30] and fumble recoveries [4] in '83 . . . Named PFWA, UPI, PFW and Football Digest all-rookie in '81 when he started the last nine games . . . Piccolo Award Winner . . . 38th player, 5th linebacker in the '81 draft.

Matt Suhey   26

Running back   Penn State
Height—5-11   Weight—216
Born—7-7-58,
State College, Pa.
Acquisition — Second-round choice in 1980 draft.
1985 season — Recorded his third NFL 100-yard game against Detroit [11-10] with 102 yards on 16 carries.
Pro career — Second-leading rusher in '84 with 424 yards on 125 carries and 4 TDs . . . Second in receptions [41] . . . Key 33-yard catch set up a touchdown in the '84 playoff victory over the Redskins . . . Caught two TD passes from Payton on a halfback option in '84 . . . Had his first 100-yard game vs. Tampa Bay [11-20-83] with 112 yards on 19 attempts . . . 7th running back selected in '80 draft, 46th player overall.

Ken Taylor   31

Cornerback   Oregon State
Height—6-1   Weight—186
Born—9-23-63,
San Jose, Calif.
Acquisition — Signed as a free agent 5-23-85.
1985 season — Picked off a Gary Hogeboom pass to set up the final touchdown vs. Dallas [11-17] . . . Began the season as a

punt and kickoff returner . . . Returned 25 punts for 198 yards and a 7.9 average . . . Longest return was 21 yards . . . Returned one kickoff for 18 yards . . . Played in all 16 games as a rookie and started against Green Bay [11-3] . . . 6 tackles and 3 interceptions.

Tom Thayer   57

Off. guard   Notre Dame
Height—6-5   Weight—268
Born—8-16-61,
Joliet, Ill.
Acquisition — Signed as a free agent.
1985 season — Received a game ball vs. San Francisco [10-13] . . . Started at right guard for the last 13 games after serving as a back-up the first three games.
Pro career — Drafted by the Bears in the 4th round of the '83 draft, but chose to join Chicago in the USFL . . . Got into 10 games as a rookie for the Blitz and started in eight games . . . Received the starting nod in the final nine games of '83, including a playoff game at Philadelphia . . . First pro start came on 5-15-83, also at Philadelphia . . . Played at left guard for Blitz after replacing Kari Yli-Renko.

Calvin Thomas 33

Running back   Illinois
Height—5-11   Weight—245
Born—1-7-60,
St. Louis, Mo.
Acquisition — Signed as a free agent 5-21-80.
1985 season — 4 touchdowns, all in the last 7 games . . . Missed two games with an injured knee.
Pro career — Shared playing time with Matt Suhey at fullback the last half of '84 . . . Had his NFL best of 57 yards on 5 carries vs. Detroit [11-18-84] . . . A 37-yard run vs. Lions also was his NFL best . . . Scored his first pro TD in the season finale at Detroit [12-16-84] . . . Valued special teams performer who forced a fumble in season opener vs. Tampa Bay [9-2-84].

Cliff Thrift   52

Linebacker   E. Centl. Oklahoma
Height—6-1   Weight—237
Born—5-3-56,
Dallas, Tex.
Acquisition — Claimed on waiv-

ers from San Diego 7-9-85.
1985 season — Played in 14 games, started 2 . . . 9 tackles, 1 sack, 1 fumble recovery and 1 pass deflection . . . Valued special teamer.
Pro career — Had career high 15 tackles at Pittsburgh in playoffs 1-9-82 . . . San Diego's third-round choice in '79 draft.

Mike Tomczak   18

Quarterback   Ohio State
Height—6-1   Weight—195
Born—10-23-62,
Calumet City, Ill.
Acquisition — Signed as free agent 5-9-85.
1985 season — Completed his first NFL pass for 24 yards to Wrightman vs. Falcons [11-24] . . . Played in six games.

Keith Van Horne   78

Off. tackle   USC
Height—6-7   Weight—280
Born—11-6-57,
Mt. Lebanon, Penn.
Acquisition — 1st round draft choice in 1981.
1985 season — Received game ball against San Francisco [10-13] . . . Has missed only six games since joining the Bears.
Pro career — Started 14 games in 1984 . . . Started 10 games in '83 before injuring his ankle vs. the Rams [11-6] . . . Consensus all-rookie choice . . . Eleventh player selected [first lineman] in the '81 draft.

Henry Waechter   70

Def. tackle   Nebraska
Height—6-5   Weight—275
Born—2-13-59,
Dubuque, Ia.
Acquisition — Signed as a free agent 12-5-84.
1985 season — 6 tackles and 2½ sacks as substitute . . . Waived 9-2, re-signed 9-4.
Pro career — Started the final two games of '84 . . . Had two sacks in the season finale vs. Detroit [12-16-84], 1 sack in the playoff victory over the Redskins . . . Played four games in '84 with the Colts before being waived.

Otis Wilson 55

Linebacker   Louisville
Height—6-2   Weight—232
Born—9-15-57,
New York, N.Y.
Acquisition — No. 1 selection in the 1980 draft.
1985 season — Pro Bowl selection...69 tackles, 11.5 sacks and 3 interceptions...Had 5 tackles, 2 sacks, 5 hurries vs. Dallas [11-17] to earn Sports Illustrated and NFC Player of the Week honors...Had his first NFL safety against the Packers [10-21].
Pro career — Enjoyed his best season as a pro, finished fifth on the team in tackles [61] and fourth in sacks [7.5]...Consistent play earned a game ball vs. Green Bay [9-16] and New Or-leans [10-7]...Had season highs of 10 tackles vs. the Rams [11-11] and two sacks vs. Detroit [12-16]...9-tackle, 1.5 sack performance vs. the Raiders [11-4]...Pulled groin vs. Seattle [9-23] and missed the following game vs. Dallas [9-30]...Team's second leading tackler in '81 [81]; third leading tackler in '83 [100] ...Had a 39-yard interception return for a TD vs. Tampa Bay [1-2-83]...Made his first pro start in the last game of his rookie season vs. Tampa Bay in place of injured Jerry Muckensturm and responded with 7 solos and an interception...First career theft came against Archie Manning [9-14-80], first sack on Gary Danielson [10-19-80]...First linebacker, 19th player selected in '80 draft.

Tim Wrightman 80

Tight end   UCLA
Height—6-3   Weight—237
Born—3-27-60,
Harbor City, Calif.
Acquisition — Signed as a free agent 3-28-85.
1985 season — Caught his first NFL touchdown pass vs. Jets [12-14]...Made his first NFL start vs. San Francisco [10-13]...Finished the preseason as the team's leading receiver with 5 catches for 107 yards and a 21.4 average.
Pro career — Originally drafted by Bears in the third round of the '82 draft...Signed with the Chicago Blitz to become first player to sign with the United States Football League.

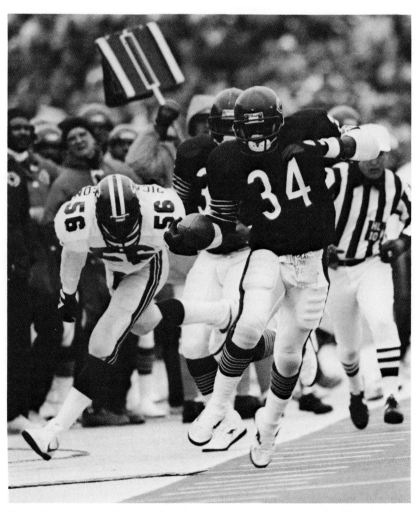

Walter Payton uses his superb balance to stay inbounds on his 40-yard touchdown run in the 36–0 victory over Atlanta on Nov. 24 at Soldier Field. (Tribune photo by Charles Cherney)

All-time Bears Team

By Don Pierson

If all the Monsters were on the same Midway, the only thing the Chicago Bears would have to fear would be George Halas himself.

"Coach Halas would welcome such a group," said all-time tight end and second-string coach Mike Ditka.

Picking the coach of the all-time Bears' team was easy. Picking the running backs wasn't.

Red Grange and George McAfee end up returning kicks and punts because Walter Payton, Gale Sayers and Bronko Nagurski won't get off the field.

"I'd have to find a place for Bill Osmanski. Halfback speed and fullback power," said all-time announcer Jack Brickhouse.

What about fullback Rick Casares? He still is second only to Payton on the all-time Bear yardage list.

"Rick played as hard as anybody I ever played with, but probably no harder than Nagurski," said Ditka.

Quarterback Sid Luckman wouldn't have to pass with Payton, Sayers and Nagurski behind him.

"Can you imagine? What a dream backfield," said Luckman.

The dream team is a product of the *Tribune*'s sports department chosen by the science of argument and designed to win games if not friends.

Longevity was important, although five-year veteran Mike Singletary was chosen and 12-year linebacker Joe Fortunato was not.

The linebacking crew contains no new-fangled "outside" linebackers. Singletary is today's middle linebacker. Bill George invented the position. Dick Butkus redefined it. Go ahead, try to run outside. Try to pass over them. Make their day.

With Doug Atkins and Dan Hampton at defensive ends, would anyone dare run outside?

Bears' founder and owner, George "Papa Bear" Halas.

"For linebackers, you've got to have Bill George, Joe Fortunato and Larry Morris as a group. The best without a doubt," said Irv Duboff, a fan who has missed no home games and only a few road games in 44 years. He stays at the Bears' hotels.

Some players were so good they could have made it on offense and defense.

Nagurski played defensive tackle as well as fullback, making him the original "Refrigerator" Perry.

"He could make any team, but I don't know what position," said Luckman.

"I wouldn't go very far now on the goal line," said Nagurski.

Grange popularized pro football with his 1925 barnstorming tour, but a 1927 injury caused him to say, "I was just another halfback after that."

George Connor made the team at offensive tackle, but said, "I think I prefer defense." He was the only player to make all-pro at both linebacker and offensive tackle for three years in a row,

1951–52–53.

"I'd be inclined to put Moose Connor on defense," said Brickhouse. "I saw him put too many people on stretchers."

Ditka and Connor both noticed that end Ken Kavanaugh was missing. Brickhouse wanted to find a place for flanker Johnny Morris. Okay, if it's ever third and long, let Morris or Kavanaugh sub for Nagurski.

Harlon Hill is the speed receiver opposite Ditka, but Morris caught more passes and Kavanaugh caught more touchdown passes.

Different eras and different rules make for different opinions.

"Teams today are far superior. They're stronger, bigger, faster and start younger," said Luckman.

"But they're no tougher now," said Grange.

Tackle Joe Stydahar measured courage by the number of missing teeth. As coach of the Rams, he demanded at halftime: "Don't call yourself a pro until you've lost at least six teeth." Then he demonstrated by removing a denture.

Guard Danny Fortmann could double as team doctor, and guard Stan Jones could double as strength coach. Fortmann earned his M.D. in mid-career. Jones was one of the first to benefit from weight training.

Center Bulldog Turner was "the smartest football player I ever knew," said Connor. "Knew every player's assignment. He played halfback once in a pre-season game."

Halas called defensive tackle Ed Healey the most versatile tackle of all time. Healey represents old-timers and the Halas penchant for spending money. He was the first player ever purchased from another team. The cost of $100 was twice the going rate for franchises.

Defensive tackle Fred Williams would keep the team loose.

"Halas traded me to Washington in 1964, and then they got

Sayers and Butkus and didn't bat .500 with them. So I always figured Sayers and Butkus didn't replace me," said Williams.

Three safeties are in the secondary—Richie Petitbon, Gary Fencik and Rosey Taylor—plus J. C. Caroline, a running back turned cornerback.

Bob Thomas broke George Blanda's placekicking records except for extra points.

"Couldn't we have George kick the extra points?" asked Brickhouse.

Bobby Joe Green punted for 35,000 yards. Payton hasn't even run that far yet.

There are 14 Hall of Fame members on the team—Halas, Atkins, Butkus, Connor, Fortmann, George, Grange, Healey, Luckman, McAfee, Nagurski, Sayers, Stydahar and Turner. Six more were left off—Blanda, triple threat Paddy Driscoll, helmetless end Bill Hewitt, defensive tackle Link Lyman, who developed the stunting style of rushing; tackle-guard George Musso, who played against Presidents Reagan and Ford; and center George Trafton, first to snap with one hand. In 12 seasons, he never made a bad snap.

Put them on special teams.

"It's impossible to pick an all-time team. There's no way," said Duboff.

How about most valuable player?

"Atkins and Butkus on defense. Payton and Luckman on offense," said Brickhouse.

"Without a doubt, Walter Payton has to be the greatest all-around back who ever walked on a football field," said Luckman.

Coach

George Halas always was reluctant to single out one Bear over another, at least in public. It would have been difficult for him to select one all-time team, but he probably would have approved of any all-time team. He called Doug Atkins the greatest defensive end he had ever seen. Since he saw them all, that was high praise. He shied away from offering comparisons between Walter Payton and Gale Sayers or between Bill George and Dick Butkus. As a judge of talent, however, Halas might have been peerless. Members of his last

championship team in 1963 credit Halas with putting the right players on the field regardless of reputation off it.

Offense

George Connor, tackle: Only player to make All-Pro at linebacker *and* offensive tackle 3 straight years, 1951–53.

Mike Ditka, tight end: Drafted out of Pitt in '61, played in 5 straight Pro Bowl games. Is 3rd on all-time Bear receptions list.

Danny Fortmann, guard: "Doctor Dan" was a 5-time All-Pro selection. Received his M.D. from U. of Chicago, 1940.

Harlon Hill, split end: From tiny Florence State Teachers College, caught 40 TD passes and averaged 20.4 yards per catch in 8 seasons [1954–61]. He was All-Pro his first three years and once caught 4 TDs in a game.

Stan Jones, guard: Drafted out of Maryland in 1954, played 12 years with Bears and participated in 7 Pro Bowls.

Sid Luckman, quarterback: In 12 seasons with the Bears [1939–50], he passed for 14,686 yards and 137 touchdowns, both club records. In his biggest year [1943], he threw 28 touchdown passes, also a club record.

Bronko Nagurski, fullback: Played 9 years with Bears, made All-Pro 3 times. All-America at Minnesota. Hall of Fame, 1963.

Walter Payton, halfback: "Without a doubt, he has to be the greatest all-around back who ever walked on a football field," says Sid Luckman.

Gale Sayers, halfback: Broke in with 22 TDs as rookie in 1965. Set 23 Bear records and 7 NFL marks. Hall of Fame, 1977.

Joe Stydahar, tackle: First player ever drafted by the Bears [1936]. All-Pro 4 times, Hall of Fame inductee in 1967.

Clyde "Bulldog" Turner, center: Played 12 seasons with Bears [1940–52], named All-Pro 6 times. Hall of Fame, 1966.

Defense

Doug Atkins, end: An intimidating 6-8 pass-rusher, played with Bears 12 years. All-Pro pick 3 times and Hall of Fame inductee

in 1982.

Dick Butkus, linebacker: Inducted into Hall of Fame in 1979, middle linebacker played 9 years with Bears and made All-Pro in 8 of them.

J. C. Caroline, cornerback: Drafted in 1956 from Illinois, played 10 years for Bears. Pro Bowl selection in 1957.

Gary Fencik, safety: In 10th year with Bears, is 2nd on club's all-time interception list. All-Pro in '79, two-time Pro Bowl selection.

Bill George, linebacker: 14-year Bear credited with "creating" middle linebacker position in 1954. Named All-Pro 8 times.

Dan Hampton, end: First-round pick out of Arkansas in 1979, he has already played in 3 Pro Bowl games. Had 11½ sacks in '84.

Ed Healey, tackle: Dartmouth product played for Bears from 1922 to 1927. Was inducted into Hall of Fame in 1964.

Richie Petitbon, safety: All-time club leader in interceptions. His interception of a Y. A. Tittle pass clinched 1963 title-game victory.

Mike Singletary, linebacker: 2nd-round pick from Baylor in '81, led club in tackles in '83 and '84. Two-time All-Pro selection.

Roosevelt Taylor, safety: Two-time Pro Bowl pick played 9 years for Bears. Had all-time club high 9 interceptions in 1963.

Fred Williams, tackle: Colorful University of Arkansas product played 12 years with the Bears [1952–63] and was a 4-time Pro Bowl selection.

Specialists

Red Grange, kickoff returner: "Galloping Ghost," the man who lent credibility to the NFL, was inducted into Hall of Fame in '63.

Bobby Joe Green, punter: Acquired from Eagles in '62 for QB Ed Brown. With Bears 12 years. Averaged 42.1 yards per punt.

George McAfee, punt returner: A Bear for 8 years; Hall of Fame, 1966. Until recently, held NFL record of 12.78 yards per return.

Bob Thomas, placekicker: With Bears 10 years, holds 6 club records, including most points, most field goals and longest FG.